The Yarnfield Yanks

The Yarnfield Yanks

The story of the main American Army Air Force Replacement Depot at Yarnfield, Stone, Staffordshire during World War II

FRAN & MARTIN COLLINS

BREWIN BOOKS

BREWIN BOOKS
19 Enfield Ind. Estate,
Redditch,
Worcestershire,
B97 6BY
www.brewinbooks.com

Published by Brewin Books 2024

A CIP catalogue record for this book is available from the British Library.

ISBN: 978-1-85858-775-2

Printed and bound in Great Britain
by 4edge Ltd.

Contents

Prologue

Yarnfield Yank

THE YARNFIELD Yank was a commemorative black and white photo booklet produced by the men of the 70th (formerly 12th) Reinforcement (originally Replacement) Depot with a headquarters based at Jefferson Hall, in Yarnfield, near Stone, Staffordshire, during World War 2. The photos included in it were taken by Sergeant James A. Freiberg during his three years at the 70th from October 1942 until October 1945.

By the beginning of November 1945, the 70th had completed its task of repatriating US airmen in the UK to the US, so it was reassigned to France, to continue its role of processing US airmen who had served on the Continent.

It was in 1945 that the booklet was completed in the photographic laboratory on base and it was printed in France. The publication was supervised

Far left: Cover of Yarnfield Yank.

Left: Major David C. Stubbs. (Yarnfield Yank)

by Major David C. Stubbs and edited by Sergeant Henry J. Swislowski. The cover was designed by Pfc David M. Clark.

In very few words, but very many photos, the booklet tells the story of the wartime journey of the men and women of the 70th and the airmen they processed.

Original copies of this 48-page booklet are hard to come by and we are indebted to Shaun Farrelly for kindly providing us with an electronic copy. A large number of the illustrations in this book come from that copy.

Chapter 1

'Better than Average Facilities'

ON 2 January 1942, shortly after the events at Pearl Harbor, the United States Eighth Air Force was formed, with its headquarters in Savannah, Georgia. On 8 January, the activation of the USAFBI (United States Army Forces in the British Isles) was announced and plans were made to transport planes and personnel of the Eighth Air Force to the UK to support the RAF in the air war against the Axis powers in Europe.

The Eighth Air Force and SOS (Services of Supply) ETOUSA (European Theater of Operations, United States of America) jointly prepared plans to cover the build up and operations of the US Army and US Army Air Forces in the UK.

Part of the plans involved setting up a system of replacement depots to provide replacement personnel for both the ground forces and the air forces based in the UK and on the Continent.

In April 1942, the 12th Replacement Control Depot was assigned to USAFBI as one of a number of units earmarked to form the Eighth Air Service Command. The 12th was to take responsibility for the receipt and processing of casual (unassigned) air force personnel arriving in Britain.

The Air Force Reinforcement (Replacement) Command operated directly under Air Forces Headquarters and had little connection to the Ground Forces Reinforcement Command, except that both were coordinated by the Replacement Section of ETOUSA Headquarters. On 27 April, advance echelons of the Eighth Air Force and Eighth Bomber, Fighter and Base Commands prepared for movement overseas. The first shipment arrived at the port of Liverpool on 11 May 1942.

On 10 June 1942, the 12th Replacement Control Depot arrived in England, where Major George D. Grubb assumed command. The unit proceeded to Bovingdon, Hertfordshire, where it performed duties for VIII Bomber Command. On 21 June, a detachment was assigned to Cheddington, Buckinghamshire, where it carried out similar duties.

On 24 June ETOUSA replaced USAFBI shortly before the assumption of the command by General Dwight D. Eisenhower. From the outset, ETOUSA intended to set up four or five sites for air force replacement depots in the UK. It required depots with 'better than average' facilities, each able to house around 1,000 casual personnel. The British Ministry of Supply suggested four sites: Howard and Beatty Halls near Stone in Staffordshire and two sites near Chorley, Lancashire: German Lane and Bamber Bridge.

All four sites had originally been built to house women working in nearby munitions plants and therefore had facilities superior to the standard purpose-built military installations.

The two halls in Stone had been built in 1938 as part of a complex of seven halls all named after Royal Navy Admirals: Howard, Beatty, Duncan, Nelson, Raleigh, Drake and Frobisher. They were built as living accommodation for female munitions workers who had relocated to the area from Woolwich to work at ROF Swynnerton.

On 6 August, the depot in German Lane, Chorley (AAF 591) was turned over to the USAAF. A detachment of the 12th RCD moved into the hostel and by 12 August, it was established as a replacement depot known as, Washington Hall, Air Replacement Center Number One. Plans were made for the receipt and care of 800 casuals by 18 August.

On 13 August, the depot at Bamber Bridge, Lancashire (AAF 569) was incorporated into the air force replacement system and became known as Adams Hall, Air Replacement Center Number Two.

On 12 September both Howard Hall and Beatty Hall were assigned to the USAAF, but were not occupied until October. The two halls were jointly known as Jefferson Hall Air Replacement Center Number Three (AAF 594). All the USAAF replacement depots were named for previous US presidents. In October 1942, Duncan Hall, which was located adjacent to Howard and Beatty, was acquired by USAAF and became part of Jefferson Hall. On 3 September 1942, Colonel Cassidy (VIII AFSC) wrote:

> "There are five replacement centers, each to function as a separate unit with accommodation for staff of one hundred and one thousand, two hundred casuals – – -. This is part of a plan to process not less than ten thousand replacements in the center of England. It is planned to set up additional replacement centers in England when sites can be obtained." (Fold 3)

On 17-18 October, Colonel Cassidy inspected the depots and was favourably impressed with the site at Yarnfield, although he felt that the

70th HQ Replacement Depot (previously 12th RCD). Duncan Hall. (Fold 3)

Duncan Hall Entrance Number 2. (Milton Cook)

Aerial view of Duncan Hall. (Fold 3)

permanent party of 14 officers and 108 enlisted men was insufficient to operate the depot. He recommended that the post should acquire an additional 22 officers and 100 enlisted men.

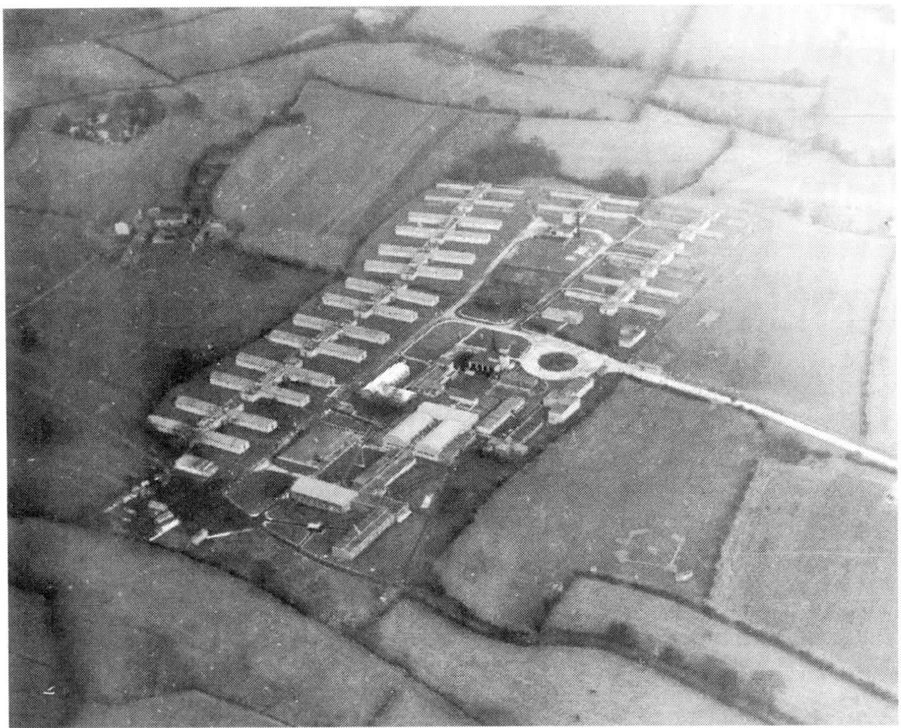

Aerial view of Beatty Hall. (Fold 3)

Beatty Hall. (Author's collection)

Flower Star at Beatty Hall. (Fold 3)

Aerial view of Howard Hall. (Fold 3)

Howard Hall. (Author's collection) (NB note incorrect spelling of Beatty on American sign)

To facilitate this, from October to November 1942, requests were made for the assignment of four replacement battalions to be assigned to the replacement depots. This would bring the potential capacity to approximately 5,000 as each battalion could handle 9,000 replacements. Unfortunately, the requests were turned down as there were no immediate plans for increasing the size of the shipments of men to the depots. In November 1942, Duncan Hall was reassigned to the jurisdiction of the Truck Transport Service of the VIII AFSC.

In January 1943, the Eighth AAF called on the VIII AFSC to justify keeping all the buildings as up to this point, they were not being used to capacity. AFSC replied:

> "The British, at great expense of time and material, have completed a programme of constructions at both Washington and Adams Hall, designed to make the three structures suitable for use of replacement centers. Additional land adjacent to the centers has been acquired and cleared for training purposes. Stations such as Washington and Adams Halls could not be duplicated under present conditions and their loss would be irreplaceable. It is recommended that Washington Hall, Adams Hall and Jefferson Hall be retained and operated by VIII AFSC as replacement centers and for such useful purposes as from time to time may arise, provided such other purposes do not interfere with the replacement center operations." (Fold 3)

The stations were retained until April 1943, when Adams Hall, which had been designated as a negro replacement center in March, was released to the Truck Transport Service in order to provide housing for Afro-American Quartermaster truck units.

On 22 April, Colonel Harvey H. Holland assumed command of the 12th Replacement Control Depot as a combined unit at its two remaining sites. Up until this point the 12th had operated as three separate units at the three separate sites, Jefferson being the headquarters. In August, Colonel Ira A. Radar assumed command. By this time demands on the replacement system had increased and the requirements for additional personnel and a stronger organization, had become acute.

*Colonel Radar's Staff. (*Yarnfield Yank*)*

Aerial view of Nelson Hall. (Fold 3)

Until June 1943, less than 4,000 men had passed through the depot, but from this time until the end of the year, there was a sudden influx of men that were needed to satisfy the demand that had arisen for replacement air troops. Due to the increase in numbers, it was proposed that all original replacement centres were restored to the replacement system.

The Truck Transport Service returned Duncan Hall to be part of the replacement system and it was incorporated back into Jefferson Hall. Nelson Hall (located in Cotes Heath) was also incorporated into Jefferson Hall. Capacity was therefore increased at Jefferson to 4,000. Adapting single beds to double deck bunks further increased the capacity to 8,000.

Nelson Hall. (Yarnfield Yank)

The request to return Adams Hall for use as a replacement depot was turned down because of the ongoing need to house Afro-American units there. Three halls near Burtonwood, Cheshire, were earmarked for the use of the replacement system to be used when required. However, the halls: Damhead, Bruche and Canada were needed instead to increase the housing capacity for Burtonwood Airfield.

The influx of large numbers of casuals during the closing months of 1943, was known as 'the Gold Rush'. During October alone, 20,000 non-assigned personnel arrived, swamping the facilities in place. Considerable negotiation and expansion of facilities was necessary to accommodate so large a number. It was also necessary to temporarily place substantial numbers of men at other stations. In late October, six extra stations were temporarily added to the system.

On 20 October 1943, 3008th, 3009th Replacement Control Depots and 3019th, and 3020th Station Complement Squadrons were assigned to Jefferson Hall. On 4 November, VIII Air Force Replacement Depot General Order Number 1 designated the 3008th and 3009th as VIII Air Force Replacement

Depot, 17th Replacement Control Depot and 3019th and 3020th as 93rd and 94th Station Complement Squadrons.

On 9 December, the 18th and 19th RCD were also assigned to Jefferson Hall. At some point the 18th was assigned to Keele Hall. On 15 December the six extra stations were released and replaced by seven different stations. Peak capacity was realised in December when 32,000 personnel were processed through the air force replacement system at one time (56,271 personnel were processed during the last few months of 1943).

Even with the extra personnel, large numbers of casuals were still needed to assist in ensuring operations continued smoothly. During the peak of operations, the permanent party personnel reached a total of 350 officers and 3,000 enlisted men, the majority of whom were casuals who had been assigned to the 12th as detached personnel.

During 1944, the system was improved and casuals arrived in smaller numbers. By 30 October, all of the replacement control depots were redesignated as Replacement Battalions (AAF) and numbered 127th-134th.

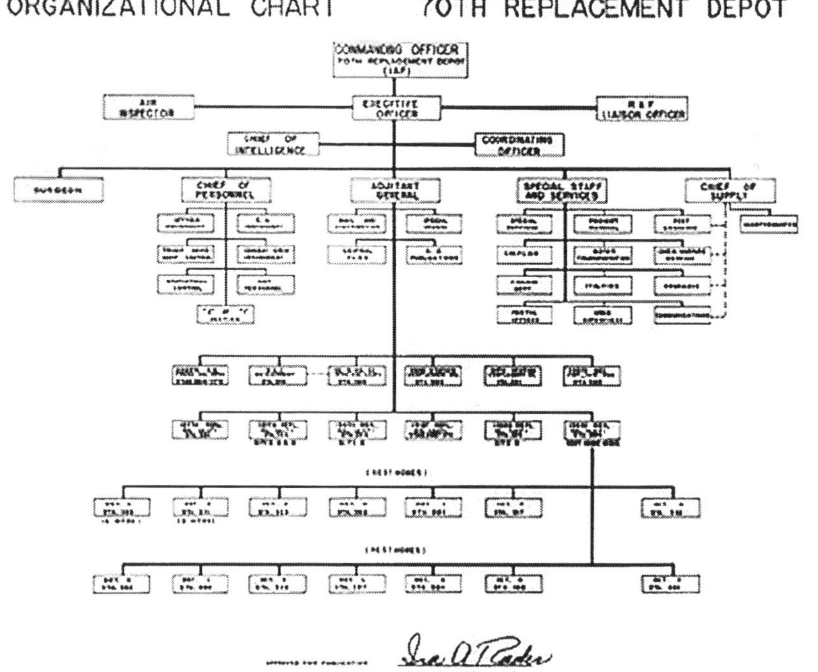

Organisational Chart. (Fold 3)

At this point the 12th Replacement Control Depot was redesignated as 70th Replacement Depot.

Part of the reason that the depot was so busy at this time was that personnel who had finished their tours were returning to the 70th to be processed for return to the US. These airmen were known as 'Happy Warriors'. At the same time the 70th was still handling personnel arriving directly from the US (known as 'Greenhorns'); personnel rotation and the reassignment of limited assignment personnel who were returning from infantry units to be attached to the air force.

In November 1944, the 128th and 134th Replacement Battalions (AAF) were sent to France and assigned to service air force units on the Continent. Advance HQ of 70th Replacement Depot was established at Bois de Boulogne, Paris, with two depots, one at Bois de Boulogne and one at Verdun.

Sometime after D-Day, all of the ground and air force replacement depots in the UK were reassigned as 'reinforcement depots' – perhaps the concept of reinforcing men in the combat zone and in the air, rather than 'replacing' them had more positive connotations.

Chapter 2

The Processing of Corporal John Jones

THE PRIMARY role of the air force replacement depot system was to process unassigned air force personnel arriving from the US and assign them to an air base. Eighty percent of personnel arriving in the UK would arrive by sea via the ports at Liverpool or Glasgow. Of the 20% arriving by air, a proportion would be passengers of Air Transport Control, and others would arrive as a complete crew, ferrying a plane over for the use of the Eighth or Ninth Air Forces in the UK. Once it had arrived in Britain, the plane would be turned over to the AAF for use wherever needed. Crews ferrying planes over would usually be assigned to a base together as a crew, rather than individually being assigned to a number of different air bases.

Aerial view of Seighford Airfield. (Alec Brew)

The depot at Yarnfield used Seighford Airfield to fly personnel in and out. Construction had begun on Seighford in 1942 and it opened in

1943 primarily as a relief landing ground for RAF Hixon (7½ miles away). During the war it was also used for RAF training and an emergency landing strip for US planes diverted by bad weather.

*Repatriates and troops arriving by air at Seighford Airfield. (*Yarnfield Yank*)*

Happy Warriors marking baggage for Zone of the Interior (USA). (Fold 3)

BARLEY

Mormons

*'A Row of Military Grips from America' – description of US airmen arriving at Jefferson Hall December 1942. (*London Daily Express *7/12/1942)*

As well as processing unassigned airmen to their designated airfields, the depot processed 'Happy Warriors' who had completed their tour of a number of missions. The number of missions required changed at various points in the war, depending on expectation of losses, actual number of losses and availability of replacements. Early in 1942, crews were expected to be in the UK for one year, after that, the number fluctuated between 25 and 35 sorties for bomber crews and 150 to 200 hours for fighter and reconnaissance pilots.

Harold Throop. (Shaun Farrelly)

Harold Throop, who worked in the Message Centre at Jefferson Hall from 1942 until 1945, recalls seeing the eager, fresh-faced young men (Greenhorns) arriving in crisp new uniforms, being processed and dispatched to their designated airfield. He also remembers seeing the difference in the faces of those passing through Jefferson Hall to return home. Having faced the pressures of warfare, they were now not so fresh-faced and their uniforms, not quite so crisp.

Combat crews going through Jefferson Hall could be processed by the replacement depots in four to five days, while replacement casuals could take five to six days. Personnel returning to the US would take up to 13 days to process. Ground force personnel were sometimes reassigned to air force units

*Harold Throop in the Message Centre where he was assigned at Jefferson Hall. (*Yarnfield Yank*)*

for various reasons. These men would often arrive at the depot with poor or incomplete records, so it would take longer to process them – up to 42 days. Limited assignment personnel might have a condition or disability as a result of an injury during combat that would limit the roles that they could be assigned to, so this group of men also took up to 42 days to process and place in a new unit.

If the men were to be assigned to the Continent, the process would take longer, as it was necessary to procure transportation (either by air or sea). Air crews were generally sent by air and ground crews by sea. As it was explained in the archives:

> "The difference is that air crews have a great deal of luggage (parachute, flying equipment etc) and if they were sent by boat, it is possible they might lose part of it and a partially equipped air crew member is of no value to the Tactical Organization." (Fold 3)

Personnel returning from the Continent were assigned to the casual pool of the 70th Reinforcement Depot. They were then directed to proceed to the 134th Reinforcement Battalion for transportation to the UK. Afro-American USAAF personnel were processed in Warrington (possibly at Bruche Hall) where arrangements had been made with a truck battalion to house and service personnel while awaiting orders.

The 70th Replacement Depot had a smooth-running system in place to process personnel as quickly and efficiently as possible. Before the arrival of the servicemen, the Chief of Transportation would receive information on the type of personnel to expect and would notify the 70th RD Headquarters at Stone, who maintained a record of all vacancies and would inform Transportation where troops should be sent. Troop Movement Control would notify all sections concerned, i.e. motor pool; site commanders where troops were to be billeted; the mess; chaplain; and medics if needed.

Upon arrival, personnel would be met at the railway station and transported to the billeting site. The majority of troop trains would arrive between midnight and 0600 hours after a long journey from the ports at either Liverpool or Glasgow. The baggage detail would have two groups of men ready, one to unload the baggage from the train and onto the trucks; the other to unload the baggage from the trucks at the post.

Stone Railway Station 2022. (M. Collins)

Buses leaving the motor pool to pick up casuals. (Fold 3)

*Troops boarding buses at Cold Meece Railway Station after disembarking. (Cold Meece Station was built by the LMS to serve ROF Swynnerton. It closed in 1959). (*Yarnfield Yank*)*

Newly arrived men boarding a bus at Cold Meece Railway Station. (Fold 3)

Casual Baggage Tent. (Fold 3)

*Stone Baggage. (*Yarnfield Yank*)*

Troops arriving at Howard Hall. (Fold 3)

*Unloading at Beatty Hall. (*Yarnfield Yank*)*

*Newly arrived casuals going to barracks. (*Yarnfield Yank*)*

Newly arrived men being billeted at Howard Hall. (Fold 3)

New arrivals get out mess kits. (Fold 3)

AUTH:
DATE:
INITIALS:

BILLETING AND HOUSING REPORT AS OF 2359 __________.
70TH REINFORCEMENT DEPOT (AAF) - AAF STA 594.

CAP	STATIONS	OCCUPANTS	COMMITTED	AVAILABLE	DEP NEXT [illegible]	ANTIC VAC
	Duncan O.					
	E.M.					
	Beatty O.					
	E.M.					
	Howard O.					
	E.M.					
	Nelson O.					
	E.M.					
	Total					

DEPARTURES:	Duncan	Beatty	Howard	Nelson	Total
Today					
Tomorrow					

ARRIVALS:					
Today					
Tomorrow					

REMARKS:

70th RD Para 14

Billeting form for 70th RD. (Fold 3)

The depots endeavoured to billet incoming troops together so once numbers had been rectified, other personnel were often required to move to other wings. Each wing of the barracks was under the charge of a Barracks Chief who would have the responsibility for keeping order, issuing passes, making bed checks, performing reveille and preparing the men for shipment.

Queue for medical check at the dispensary at Duncan Hall. (Fold 3)

Medical Staff. (Fold 3)

The following day, processing would begin. This would consist of a medical examination, orientation talks on chemical warfare, training on ordnance and a visit to the chaplain if required. New personnel would be shown the film: *Welcome to Britain* and be given a brief outline of social expectations in England. There would also be a lecture on security and finally, American dollars would be exchanged for British sterling.

Before the men left the depot, clothing checks were carried out to ascertain if each man had the necessary equipment and clothing for his assignment. This could lead to delays if the quartermaster was short of some items of stock. While the men were at the replacement depot, they would be expected to carry out various duties and details.

*Quartermaster Staff. (*Yarnfield Yank*)*

Finance Section. (Fold 3)

Personnel Section. (Fold 3)

*Utilities Staff. (*Yarnfield Yank*)*

Once the personnel had been fully processed, Troop Motor Control would consult the train schedule and notify the depot when the move could take place. Motor pool, mess and other concerned departments would be informed and personnel would be trucked or marched to the railway station. At Yarnfield, the motor pool was located within the Duncan Hall site but served all of Jefferson Hall.

Motor Pool. (Fold 3)

RTO Staff. (Yarnfield Yank)

Switchboard Operators. (Yarnfield Yank)

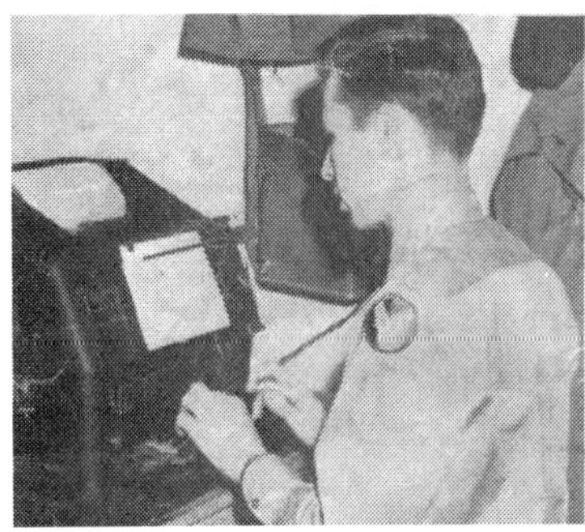

Teletype Operator. (Yarnfield Yank)

Special Orders. (Yarnfield Yank)

Communications Staff. (Yarnfield Yank)

Classification Staff. (Yarnfield Yank)

Classification Office. (Yarnfield Yank)

TJA Staff. (Yarnfield Yank)

HQ & 93rd Station Complement Squadron. (Yarnfield Yank)

*Officers at Yarnfield. (*Yarnfield Yank*)*

The following passage provided by the 70th Replacement Depot illustrates the journey of the fictional character, Corporal John Jones, through the processing system.

"Arrival and Activities on the Post of a typical enlisted man:

The majority of troop trains arrive between midnight and 0600 hours, after a very long trip from some port in the north. Corporal John Jones, who will serve as our typical soldier arriving in England, pulls into the station tired, dirty and not having eaten a hot meal in twenty-four hours. One or two of his companions may have become ill on the journey and on debarking from the train these men are sent to the dispensary in an ambulance which has been provided by the Medical Department for such an emergency. Jones and the rest of the movement board trucks or buses and proceed to the post. Here they are guided to the auditorium and seated to await the preparation of the billeting forms, which are made out in duplicate for such arriving enlisted men. During this waiting period, Corporal Jones, intensely interested in being overseas, is full of all the questions that occur to newly arrived troops in England and though he would hesitate to ask most officers, since they are all involved in the troop movement, he is glad to see that the chaplain is there to answer anything he might want to ask.

Soon his turn comes to have his billeting slip completed and he is escorted through the blackout to his room and, after washing, is taken to the mess hall where there is a hot meal awaiting him. Finally, he goes to bed in a room with three others and is not disturbed until he has had a good sleep.

Corporal Jones spends his first day on the post in orientation and inspections which have been carefully scheduled prior to his arrival. The first formation is a routine physical examination where particular attention is paid to contagious diseases which may have been contracted on the journey. After the physical examination, Jones has a brief free moment in which to pick up his bags at the baggage tent before he goes to the auditorium for the most important part of his stay on the post, the orientation lecture. On the way to the lecture, he drops his ammunition with the Ordnance Officer, as he has been instructed to do by the Barracks Chief.

After a brief word of greeting from the Commanding Officer, the main part of the orientation lecture begins with the talk by the Adjutant who opens with an explanation to the men of the general purpose of the command and the reason for their being there, namely, to be assigned to a position in the Air Force. Conduct on the post is then dealt with, particular emphasis being given to the care of the post and the fact that it must be turned back to the British in a good or better condition than it was when the United States Army took it over. The general question of economy incident to being in a theater of operations is then discussed and soldiers are told of the regulations appertaining to the use of hot water, salvaging razor blades and tin cans and especially the saving of food, of which they are told there is enough to satisfy their appetite, but not enough to allow any waste. The fact that they are now within a very short distance from the enemy is stressed and precautions in connection with this are reviewed, particularly preservation of the natural camouflage; individual responsibilities in case of air raid; gas alarm; airborne attack; preservation of blackout; and giving of alarms in case of fire. Each individual is then urged to be thorough and conscientious in everything he does, or is about to do, in view of the coming assignment in this theater of operations which is in direct contact with the enemy and needs the very best work that each man can offer. This portion of the orientation closes with a strong emphasis on military courtesy and the standards that it is based upon in this theater.

The next talk is given by the Public Relations Officer who opens with a description of certain English customs, manners of approach and intuitions which are strikingly different from ours, and urges that the individual American bear in mind when he is amused by these differences that they are part of the heritage of English civilizations, that he is to some extent the guest of the English, and that he should conduct himself accordingly. The soldiers are reminded that the English form their opinion of the whole American Army by the individual American soldiers whom they see, and a plea is made to the men's pride to bear this in mind in connection with their personal appearance, drinking, manner with civilians and general behavior. The soldiers are reminded that they are the highest paid and best fed soldiers in the world and that in direct contrast, the English have been rationed in food and drink for four years and have a very much lower wage level than ours. In connection with this contrast, the men are told not to spend lavishly, not to buy bottles of liquor in pubs, not to display a big 'roll', and never attempt to show friendship by buying an Englishman, who feels bound to reciprocate, a lot of drinks. Those who possess knives with blades over three inches in length are told that they must hand them in to the Adjutant's office. The lack of color line in England is the last question dealt with by the Public Relations Officer and he treats this at great length, realizing that it is in very sharp contrast to the attitude in the States and a fact that can lead to a great amount of trouble if the men are not conscious of it when they leave the post.

The Security Officer is the next speaker and opens his talk with a discussion of the great importance of becoming 'Security-minded'. He explains that although censorship is rigorous, its ultimate success depends upon the sense of responsibility of the individual to protect information that would aid the enemy. Soldiers are asked to fight the urge to discuss the units in which they take very natural pride, because of the fact that each little bit of information, no matter how insignificant it may seem, has a part in the big jigsaw puzzle that enemy intelligence tries to assemble. An explanation of the regulations governing the whole question of mail censorship and what constitutes the violation of these regulations closes the talk by the Security Officer.

The Medical Officer has a few words of warning to say concerning the lack of sanitary standards in pubs and restaurants, and the variation in weather necessitating warm dress. He also speaks of the soldier's responsibility for keeping clean, for ventilating his room and for drinking only water marked 'Drinking Water'. He urges everyone to report to the dispensary at the slightest suggestion of sickness and above all, not to attempt to treat himself. Most emphasis is placed on the question of venereal disease and the extreme importance of stamping it out in a theater of operations where man hours are lost, are doubly important. Weapons for the fight against venereal disease are described at length including prophylactic stations, V-Packets and condoms. Above all, a plea is made for continence.

The orientation lectures are closed by the Chaplain who describes the religious activities on the post and emphasizes their importance. He then makes a plea for the respect of English women, pointing out the fact that war, the breaking up of homes and expansion of industry led to a great deal of promiscuity, but that should not lead Americans to put all English women in the same category. He asks that soldiers conduct themselves as they would want Tommies to conduct themselves in relations with American girls were they stationed in the States. The Chaplain ends his talk by asking that the diversion of arrival in a new land should not draw them away from consideration of their spiritual life.

Following the indoctrination lecture which takes about an hour, Jones is free for the rest of the day to become settled on the station and make use of the facilities provided for this purpose. The Barracks Chief, as instructed, has posted in the billet a listing of all these facilities and how they should be utilized. Jones's first concern is about his mail, and he is told that he must send in his address cards to the postal office. There are some supplies such as soap and toothpaste which he needs badly, but he cannot get them until he has had his money changed. The Finance Officer has provided an opportunity to change money during the day and Jones, after changing his money, then proceeds to the post exchange to pick up his supplies. In the hall adjoining the PX is a representative of the Commercial Cable Company, through whom it is possible to cable home, which everyone is anxious to do. Since he is now overseas and very proud of it, Jones wants to be the best looking soldier he possibly can, and so he takes his clothes to be pressed and mended by the tailor, and has his hair cut by the post barber, facilities for both of which are provided by the post exchange. Any shortages of equipment are filled and Jones is ready to start working and training.

The following morning, at formation, Jones finds that about half of his group is sent out on detail and the other half is assigned to training. He is told that this procedure is followed each day and that every effort is made to alternate men daily on work detail and training. To those chosen for work, a great variety of jobs are allotted, including the old standby of KP and general policing, besides such work as construction of paths between billets and unloading dirt from trucks for fill and other jobs being carried out by the Utilities Office. The following day Jones is put in the training group and he finds that the emphasis is placed very strongly on putting him back into good physical condition after his ocean voyage, and on reviewing basic training on which he, along with many of his companions, had become very rusty. To fill the former purpose, there are classes in calisthenics, which increase in difficulty the longer he stays on the post; many group games such as basketball, touch football, softball and baseball; and finally long road marches with and without equipment. As far as his basic training is concerned, the stress is laid primarily on checking gas equipment, field demonstration of gasses and a trip through the gas chamber. Although he was issued a carbine in the States, Jones has never learned the manual of the piece, nor its nomenclature, nor how to field strip it, and he receives instruction in all of these points. He also gets a refresher course in military courtesy and discipline and close-order drill, supplemented by training films on these subjects. Two formal retreats are held each week and Saturday morning inspection is very strict and takes a great deal of preparation.

During his off-duty hours, Jones has a great deal to occupy his time. There are two showings each night of a motion picture in the post auditorium. This routine is broken each week by a dance held in the auditorium on Saturday nights. Every now and then a stage show comes to the post from the USO circuit. There are also dances at least once a week at a neighboring hostel given by the girls at the Royal Ordnance Factory or at a WREN or WAAF station. There is a Saturday night liberty run to Hanley. Nearby pubs provide an escape from the routine of the post and give Jones his first chance to meet and become acquainted with the English. Athletic equipment and books are available at all times at the Special Service Office and the Red Cross provides a luxurious lounge and snack bar. The lounge has pool tables, ping-pong equipment, a good library, a phonograph and many records, magazines and a piano. The snack bar is open until 2130 hours and the lounge until 2300 hours.

Religious services are provided regularly and for all denominations. Jones soon becomes acquainted with the Chaplain and finds that he is at his office at all times ready to talk with Jones or any of his buddies. Jones also takes advantage of arrangements that are made to have soldiers attend services at local churches. The Red Cross Field Director is also on tap to help solve any personal problems.

Departure:

> While Jones is involved in his work and recreation, orders are issued for his transfer to his first permanent station in the ETO. These orders, together with outgoing troop movement orders are received at the Adjutants Office. The mess is immediately notified of how many men there will be for whom early breakfast and sandwiches for the journey must be prepared. The Surgeon is notified and he releases all men on this order who have minor ailments or notifies the Adjutant of men who will have to be scratched from the shipment pending recovery. The Barracks Chief is notified of the movement and he in turn notifies the men of their time of departure. Each men's helmet and leggings are marked with the movement number. Rations are issued to the men, C rations if the journey covers two or more meals, and sandwiches if it takes only one meal. Along with the rest of the shipping, Jones meets a formation held by the shipping department at which his name, rank and serial number is checked against that on the orders to assure that no mistake is made on the movement. If any men miss the shipment, their names are sent to the headquarters' Personnel Officer. The trucks are loaded and the men leave AAF Stn 594 on their way to do a job for the Air Force in this Theater." (Fold 3)

There were some differences in the way officers and enlisted men were treated during the processing. The replacement depots made:

> "- - - an effort to avoid the 'herding' of officers as much as possible. Tremendous housing and feeding problems and the necessity to know where each officer is at all times, makes this very difficult to accomplish, but everything is done to make the officer feel that he is an individual receiving individual attention." (Fold 3)

Officers were not billeted in groups (as the enlisted men were). They were assigned to a company occupied on a single site. All directions and answers to queries came directly from the Adjutant's Office:

"This avoids the natural resentment an officer has at being told what to do by an enlisted man appointed as a barracks chief." (Fold 3)

Adjutant General's Staff. (Yarnfield Yank)

Adjutant General's Office. (Yarnfield Yank)

Duties of casual officers while at a replacement depot would include censorship of enlisted men's mail. Some officers would also be detailed to meet incoming shipments of men at the ports and others would be responsible for outgoing troop movements.

On base, a number of facilities were provided for casual officers. There was an officers' lounge, which was a large room where officers could read, write or talk and a bar which served beer from 10.00 to 11.30 each evening. There was also a clubroom which would be open all day. Here the men could play ping-pong, pool or darts. Each afternoon, there was a showing of the evening movie specifically for officers.

Newly arrived officers receiving orders. (Fold 3)

Richard and Heber Butler were brothers from Utah who arrived at Yarnfield in 1942 as sergeants awaiting promotion to officers so that they could pilot fighter planes. They had enlisted on the same day, in July 1940, before the US joined the war, with a view to flying Spitfires. After basic training, they boarded the Queen Elizabeth in November 1942 to sail to the UK. On 30 November, the Queen Elizabeth docked at Greenock in Scotland and the men then travelled by train to Stone. While at Jefferson Hall, the brothers were interviewed by a journalist for the *London Express*. The article was printed on 7 December 1942. Possibly the interest in the men was the fact that they had enlisted together and were both elders of the Mormon Church.

Older brother, Richard, describes in his journal, the processing that the men went through at Jefferson Hall. Of the security briefing he wrote:

> "The Colonel told it to us straight from the shoulder all about the way things got out both innocently and otherwise. And about the punishment men have received who were turned in or overheard by the authorities when they talked too much. I shouldn't have much trouble trying to keep from talking. I'm too quiet even when I'm trying to talk."
> (*P-38 Odyssey* – Dick Butler)

The brothers spent around a month at Yarnfield, which included a pass to London. They found their time at Jefferson Hall tedious and England's climate dismal. Richard writes in his journal on 5 December:

Richard and Heber Butler. (Butler family collection)

> "This English weather kills me. One minute it will be raining and the next, the sun will really be making up time lost. Don't believe it tho' cause it'll be raining again in ten minutes. The sun never gets higher than a 30 degree angle from the earth any time of the day. I've only seen it three times since I landed, so I don't much care if it doesn't even come up." (*P-38 Lightning* – Dick Butler)

And on 26 December, he wrote:

> "I've come so damn near freezing to death since I landed that it isn't funny. It's naturally about ten degrees too cold for comfort in the rooms and the air is .9 water, which makes it worse. Coats don't do any good." (*P-38 Lightning* – Dick Butler)

In a V-mail he writes on the subject of how he feels about his time at the replacement depot awaiting processing:

MORMONS PREFER SPITFIRES

Express Staff Reporter

TO a U.S. Air Corps station yesterday came two young men with a double faith—the brothers Butler, elders of the Mormon Church, fighter pilots of the American Army.

Richard Marsh Butler is 23. Heber Marsh Butler is 21. They come from their society's famous centre and home of its Temple—Salt Lake City, Utah.

And the brothers Butler, elders of the Latter Day Saints, want above all else to get cracking in a Spitfire apiece.

The Mormon fighters think there is something about a Spitfire.

They had just arrived at an Air Corps Replacement Centre with a bunch of U.S. sergeant pilots—the first to reach Britain.

They all talk about their American Thunderbolts and Lightnings. Maybe some day, they say, they will have something as good as the Spitfire. It seems, however, they want to fly Spitfires right now.

1886, AGED 6

"Say," said Elder Richard Marsh Butler, "do you know anyone around London name of Marsh?"

His mother's name is Marsh. She left England in 1886, aged six. Her sons would like to trace the family.

"Our mother married into the faith of the Church of Jesus Christ of Latter Day Saints," said Richard, "our father is a High Priest of the Mormon Church, and one brother is a bishop.

"Heber and I joined up on the same day, in July 1940. Heber started to take flying lessons before he was old enough to join."

Richard was married at Salt Lake City Temple this year and Heber at another Mormon church.

Neither of the brothers smokes, drinks, or takes tea or coffee. Heber carries in his flying coat pocket his Articles of Faith.

Number 10 says: "We believe—that the earth will be renewed and receive its paradisiacal glory."

Elder Heber considers that is not a bad thing to carry in a Spitfire.

London Daily Express.
(7/12/1942)

> "It's beginning to get pretty dull around here, a good rest was just what I needed, but for me, I've had about enough. I'm ready to get back on the job any day now. There's no place to go around here to enjoy oneself, so I guess I'll take up knitting." (*P-38 Lightning* – Dick Butler)

And at another time he writes:

> "Things are getting boring every day it seems, either that, or I'm getting fed up with sitting around."

Eventually, while at Stone, on 20 December, the two men were discharged from the army and became civilians for 24 hours before taking the oath on 21 December to be sworn in as Flight Officers so they could start:

> "Living and acting as near like officers as it is possible at such short notice." (*P-38 Lightning* – Dick Butler)

Within three months, the brothers would be eligible to become 2nd Lieutenants.

On 28 December, the Butlers finally left Yarnfield, for Atcham to begin their pilot training on P-39 Airacobras and P-38 Lightnings. A month later, after training and a voyage to Oran, Algiers, they commenced flying as part of the 82nd Fighter Group.

It wasn't only US Servicemen who were processed at Jefferson Hall. In July 1943, 557 women of the first separate battalion of WAACS to land in the UK, arrived at Stone. The group were welcomed at the port of debarkation by WAAC Commander in the ETO, Captain Anna Wilson and the group's

Commanding Officer, Captain Mary A. Halleren, who, with several other officers and five enrolled members, had preceded the group to the UK. The women were part of the largest of the two WAAC expeditionary forces that had been sent to serve overseas from the US at this point. The other group had been assigned to North Africa. The girls in the group were aged 21-45 and represented all the 48 states of the US.

The group entrained from the post of debarkation and after some hours, arrived at Stone Railway Station where, within 12 minutes, packs had been adjusted and the platform was cleared. The women marched to the barracks where they were greeted by a drum and bugle corps band from the 10th Replacement Depot in Lichfield, who played *Let me call you Sweetheart* and were met with a rousing welcome from the group of men on duty. A hot meal awaited the women in the mess hall.

Wave-weary WAACs, although their GI ensembles don't show it, head for barracks, somewhere in England, to take up duties with the Eig h Air force. And they're all in step.

Stars and Stripes *20/7/1943.*

FIRST AMERICAN WACS IN BRITAIN

(Continued from Page 1)

"We know what we're fighting for," American soldiers said as they waited eagerly to handle the W. A. C.s' baggage at trains which unloaded them in the countryside where they will remain for several days' orientation before being assigned to bomber and fighter stations.

"The way they can march and maneuver, ought to make us ashamed of ourselves; they've got rhythm, those gals," the boys said as they watched the W. A. C.s in a retreat parade.

It's a Great War

"Oh, boy; oh, boy, it's a great war; British girls are nice, but there's nothing like an American girl," the American soldiers said as they flocked to a dance for the W. A. C.s and joyously sought out girls from their own states.

Already calling themselves G. I. Jeannes, the W. A. C.s are settling down to their new jobs with bubbling enthusiasm. They have undergone long and strenuous training, "almost like the Commandos," and they are eager to expend their pent-up energy in something that will help win the war as soon as possible.

The first W. A. C. to go ashore was Battalion First Sergt. Virginia M. Rosekrans, Chicago. The first W. A. C. topkick ever seen in England she regrets she didn't think up something more deathless to say when she touched shore.

"'Well, here we are,' I said, and that wasn't so hot,?" she recalled.

She's The Happiest

W. A. C. Mary Elizabeth Eliott, Kinston, N. C., is probably the happiest girl among them all. She looked up at a dance on her second night ashore here and saw her fiance, Sergt. Wallace Best, Ra-

Stars and Stripes *20/7/43. (D. Beeby)*

Lipstick Drill Comes to the ETO

Stars and Stripes *20/7/1943.*

WAAC casuals arriving at Jefferson Hall. (Fold 3)

War Not Big News in England— It's Landing of American Wacs

ANNE L. PENNICK

Called 'Angels in Khaki' by U. S. Soldiers Who Greet Them

Copyright, 1943, Chicago Daily News, Inc.

Somewhere in England, July 22. (CDN) — The bombing of Rome is not the biggest news of the moment for American troops based in England. It's the landing here of 557 American Wacs.

They are to serve as stenographers, telephone operators, drivers, cooks and communications specialists in the United States army's Eighth air force, relieving 557 men for more active duty.

"They're angels in khaki; now

(Please turn to Page 9, Column 5)

4 Wichita Girls

Four Wichita girls were among the first 557 W. A. C.s who landed in England. They were Johnnie Pennington, daughter of Mr. and Mrs. John Pennington, 905 North Waco; Anne L. Pennick, daughter of Mr. and Mrs. S. E. Pennick, 409 East Central; Laura B. Longenecker and Mary A. Wallace, street addresses unknown.

Miss Pennington enlisted in the W. A. C. last April 1. She had formerly been a long distance telephone operator for Southwestern Bell Telephone Company.

Miss Pennick was formerly secretary to Dr. Paul Carson at the Children's Clinic and enlisted last January.

Wichita newspaper July 1943. (Anne Pennick Collection, D. Beeby)

Anne Pennick wearing early WAAC dress hat. (Anne Pennick Collection, D. Beeby)

Anne Pennick wearing Men's overseas hat. (WAC overseas hat was introduced in 1944) (Anne Pennick Collection, D. Beeby)

Newly arrived WAACs being billeted. (Fold 3)

*WAAC Retreat. (*Yarnfield Yank*)*

The group had been assigned to the UK to release male airmen from the Eighth Army Air Force who had been carrying out clerical duties for combat duty. The girls faced a week being processed at Yarnfield before being assigned to air force units as stenographers, telephonists and plotters at operational stations. A number would be sent to Signal Corps School to study British operations and procedures. One of the girls was Anne Pennick, who appeared in her local paper back home.

On one of the evenings, a dance was organised for enlisted men and enrolled WAACs with an orchestra from the 10th Replacement Depot. At the dance, the girls had their first experience of English beer.

Shortly after this, on 19 August 1943, the enrolled members of the WAAC officially dropped the 'Auxiliary' in their title and became the Women's Army Corps, which meant that they were now part of the army for the duration of six months. By the end of August, all WAAC officers had also been transferred into the Women's Army Corps.

WAACs receiving orientation. (Fold 3)

WAACs Now WACs; Official Last Midnight

The WAACs officially dropped an "A" at midnight last night to become WACs—members of the Women's Army Corps of the U.S. Army, in for the duration and six months.

The conversion in the ETO became complete yesterday when a cable arrived from the War Department confirming the appointment of all ETO officers, except one. 1/Lt. Catherine Falvey, a Massachusetts state legislator, did not apply, and plans to return home.

Conversion of the last WAAC enlisted members over here was completed Aug. 19, 12 days ahead of schedule.

Stars and Stripes *1/9/1943.*

T5 Margaret L. Simmons of Bend, Oregon and Captain Marie G. Curry of Yelm, Washington patrolling on MP duty 20/7/1943.

"Dress right – dress" in preparation for the oath in to the US Army. (Anne Pennick collection, D. Beeby)

15 August, 1943 – Taking the oath into the US Army – Lt. Berry, CO Major Bostick, administering the oath, and Lt. Marble, 2nd Lt. (Anne Pennick Collection, D. Beeby)

Chapter 3

Washington Hall AAF 591

NAMED AFTER the first president of the United States, the building, originally known as 'German Lane Camp', was built to house the woman munitions workers from ROF Chorley. On 10 May 1942, the British Ministry of Works began work to develop it into a replacement centre for the USAAF and on 6 August, it was handed over to the American forces, its new title being: Washington Hall, Air Replacement Center Number One. The lane the depot stood in became known as Washington Lane.

Guardroom at Washington Hall 1944. (Euan Withersby)

Aerial photo of Washington Hall 1940s. (Lancashire County Council)

The 100 men and women who were reassigned to Washington Hall from the 12th RCD at Bovingdon and Cheddington, were led by Colonel William A. Gayle of Montgomery, Alabama (later to become Mayor of Montgomery). Washington Hall was later to become known as part of the 70th Replacement Depot and the headquarters of the 127th Reinforcement Battalion.

The base was to provide orientation, training and equipment for 1,200 casual replacements at a time arriving from the US, and also to process those men returning to the US after they had completed their tours. In fact, over 50,000 casuals passed through Washington Hall as the photo in the *Yarnfield Yank* shows. WAC casuals were also processed at Washington Hall. The base also dealt with the reassignment of US airmen serving in the air forces of other countries – primarily RAF and RCAF – to USAAF.

In 1939, when Britain declared war on the Axis forces, a number of Americans (many from British heritage) crossed the border into Canada where they were able to join the RCAF or travelled to Britain to join the RAF. When the US joined the war on the side of the Allies at the end of 1941, many of these men wanted to serve in their own country's armed forces. As

COLONEL GAYLE PINS EAGLES ON « COLONEL » GEHL
50 THOUSANDTH MAN TO PASS THROUGH CHORLEY

(*Yarnfield Yank*)

well as the patriotic reasons for wanting to serve one's own country in war, another advantage of this transfer was that the pay was better. A further gain for the American airman was that an enlisted RAF serviceman could often transfer to being an officer in the USAAF because of his flying experience.

One American, who went through this process at Washington Hall, was Joseph W. Roundhill. He had been born in Seattle, Washington, to English parents. In the 1930s, during the Depression, his mother took Joseph and his two siblings and returned to England. As soon as he was of age, he enlisted in the RAF as an under-training pilot. In 1943 he undertook orientation training at Chorley to become part of the USAAF. After this, he was assigned to the Eighth Army Air Forces Headquarters at Bushey Park G2 Intelligence.

There was a tradition amongst the USAAF that after a serviceman had been promoted to officer, he would give the first person who saluted him $10. Milton Cook (an MP from Jefferson Hall, on temporary duty at Washington Hall) was offered a 10 dollar bill by a group of such men. He ignored it and walked past as he thought he was being offered a bribe to look the other way for some misdemeanour. Later, when he found out about the tradition, he wished he had taken the money.

There were a number of activities both on and off the base for both the casuals and the permanent party at Washington Hall. The base had a dance

*MPs at Washington Hall. (*Chorley Guardian and Leyland Advertiser *via Stuart Clewlow)*

hall and cinema facilities. Special Service provided extensive sports facilities. The men were able to take part in basketball, gymnastics, volleyball, tennis and baseball. The depot had two baseball teams: The Washington Hall Yankees; and the Washington Hall Cubs. Special Service also organised tours of the local towns, e.g. Liverpool.

Dance Hall at Washington Hall. (Stuart Clewlow)

*Dance at Washington Hall. (*Yarnfield Yank*)*

There was also an American Red Cross Aero Club with lounge, games room and a library on base. The American Red Cross also had a clubmobile called Albama, that was dedicated at Washington Hall on 9 April 1943. In 1944, a 'Donut Dugout' was opened by the Red Cross in St Thomas's Road, Chorley. It was staffed by local residents. The Donut Dugout was the venue for the wedding reception of Miss Carol Lee Davis who was the American Red Cross Director on the base and Captain Ernest J. Hart who was also based at Washington Hall. They were married in uniform at Park Road Methodist Church in Chorley. The service was conducted jointly by the Reverend E.T. Wood and the chaplain from the base, Captain C. Pease. The American Red Cross Field Director for the area, Henry Day, gave the

Chorley's First All-American Wedding

HART—DAVIS

Believed to be the first all-American wedding in Chorley, took place at Park Road Methodist Church on Wednesday morning. The bride was Miss Carol Lee Davis, elder daughter of Mr. and Mrs. Frank G. Davis of Lewisburg, Pa., and the bridegroom Capt. Ernest J. Hart, U.S.A., A.G.D., youngest son of Mr. A. F. Hart of Asheville, North Carolina.

The couple met when both were stationed at Washington Hall, Chorley, where the bride is American Red Cross Club Director. Both were in uniform at the wedding as was the bride's Red Cross colleague, Programme Director Miss Margaret Kennedy of Iowa, who was bridesmaid.

Henry Day, American Red Cross Field Director, Washington Hall, gave the bride away and Capt. O. W. Crouch, U.S.A.A.F., was best man.

The Rev. E. T. Wood and Capt. C. Pease (U.S.A.) conducted the ceremony, at which Sgt. Milton sang "Because" and "I'll Walk Beside You." Miss B. Wilkinson was organist.

After a reception at the "Do-Nut Dugout" the couple left for a honeymoon in the Lake District.

Chorley Guardian and Leyland Advertiser *10/8/1945. (via Stuart Clewlow)*

bride away. One of the enlisted men from Washington Hall, Sergeant Milton, sang *Because* and *I'll Walk Beside You* at the ceremony. After the reception, the couple spent their honeymoon in the Lake District. The ceremony was believed to be the first 'All-American' wedding in Chorley.

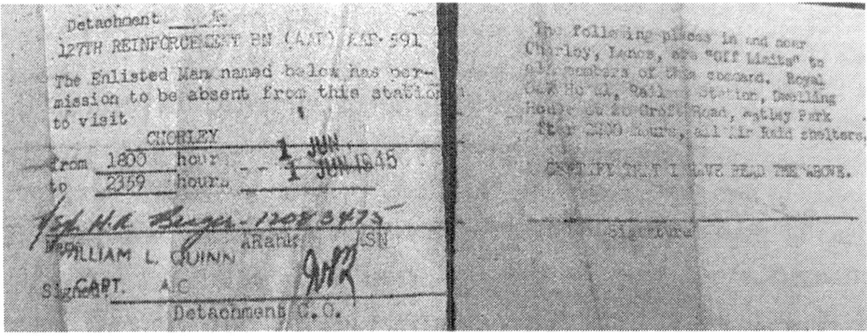

Detachment
127TH REINFORCEMENT BN (AAF) APO 591
The Enlisted Man named below has permission to be absent from this station to visit
CHORLEY
from 1800 hour 1 JUN
to 2359 hours 1 JUN 1945
Name WILLIAM L. QUINN Rank ASN
Signed CAPT. AC
Detachment C.O.

The following places in and near Chorley, Lancs, are "Off Limits" to all members of this command. Royal Oak Hotel, [illegible] Station, [illegible] [illegible] Road, [illegible] Park after 2300 hours, all Air Raid shelters.
[illegible] THAT I HAVE READ THE ABOVE.
Signature

Pass. (Stuart Clewlow)

One of the first activities the men took part in 'off-base' was a Thanksgiving service at the nearby St Laurence's Church in November 1942. The men also enjoyed frequenting the local pubs, with the exception of a number that were 'off-limits'. Apparently The Royal Oak was put off-limits to US troops when the CO, Colonel Gayle, was refused a second cup of coffee there late one evening. Although Colonel Gayle was later said to have changed his mind, the landlord decided to institute his own ban on US troops.

At some point, while the American servicemen were based at Washington Hall, a ship's wooden figurehead mysteriously appeared and remained as part of the décor. Conjecture was that a group of servicemen had brought it back from Liverpool docks. After the war, the figurehead was gifted to the Merseyside Marine Museum, which provided a fiberglass copy that was then mounted outside the building, but has since been displayed inside.

*Ship's figurehead (*Yarnfield Yank*)*

Chapter 4

Adams Hall AAF 569 (and the Battle of Bamber Bridge)

ADAMS HALL, Air Replacement Center Number Two, in Mounsey Road, Bamber Bridge, Lancashire, was the second depot to be activated by the 12th RCD on 13 August 1942. It was named after the US's second president. From March 1943, it was used as a replacement centre for Afro-American air force servicemen.

*HQ at Adams Hall. (*Yarnfield Yank*)*

In April 1943, Adams Hall was released to the Truck Transport Service in order to provide housing for Afro-American quartermaster truck units. It was while the base was used for billeting the 1511th QM Trucking Company that the infamous 'Battle of Bamber Bridge' took place in June 1943. The 'battle' was the climax of racial tension between members of the 1511th and white MPs of the 234th MP Battalion located on the other side of town.

*Adams Hall Guardhouse. (*The Battle of Bamber Bridge – *D. Rogerson)*

Although during World War Two, there was not a policy of racial discrimination in the US Army, there was a policy of 'segregation' brought into being because of conflict between white and Afro-American soldiers. As much as possible, white and black servicemen were kept separate and military units were either all black (with some white officers) or all white.

On bases that had both black and white units there were separate billets, mess halls and other facilities. Some airfields that housed white flying crews and black construction engineer units, struggled to provide equal but separate facilities for both black and white personnel.

In 1941, before American troops landed in Britain, the black population of the UK was around 8,000-10,000, a comparatively small number compared with the US. Although it had been involved in the slave trade, as had the US, it did not have the same history and colour bars that parts of the US had. The US military archives comment that:

> "Often white and negro soldiers were inevitably thrown together in social structures which would not have occurred in the United States. The frequent inability or unwillingness of many white soldiers, particularly those from the South, to recognize that negroes were merely exercising their legal privileges accorded them by British law and the US Army - - - occasionally led to outbursts which caused injuries and damage and intensified already uneasy relationships." (Fold 3)

In a report into the affair at Bamber Bridge, Colonel Grubb, who was now Commanding Officer of the Combat Support Wing – the umbrella organisation which included the trucking companies, commented on the sort of incidents that black soldiers were routinely encountering in Bamber Bridge before events led to violence.

> "Three (black) soldiers went to town with passes to go to a dance. They had dates with some girls - - - They were stopped three times by MPs asking for their passes. Finally, a 2nd Lieutenant told them, 'You soldiers don't belong here, just get out of town on the train.' After this, they went home very much disturbed and angry at their treatment. They went to their company commander." (Fold 3)

Fortunately, Colonel Grubb happened to be on the base at the time and he was able to apologise to the men for the unseemly behaviour of the white officer. He commended them for their great control and for not taking the matter into their own hands. Unfortunately, he was not on hand to calm matters down during the Bamber Bridge incident.

To understand why events escalated as they did, it is important to recognise that it was set in the aftermath of a major race riot in Detroit in the US, which had happened two days earlier. Nine white and 25 Afro-Americans had been killed. A civilian report in the US military archives states:

> "The Bamber Bridge incident of June 1943 started as an attempt by several negro soldiers to resist arrest by a white MP for being out of uniform and not having passes and culminated in a shooting affray between a handful of negro soldiers and a number of MPs in the town of Bamber Bridge, Lancashire. Unfounded rumours of the massacre of negro soldiers caused the men to arm themselves for defense and rumors of the massacre of negro troops brought an MP armored car and additional MPs to Bamber Bridge. One negro soldier was killed, several negroes and MPs were wounded and one white officer of a negro company was shot in the leg. Thirty-five negro soldiers were tried for violation of the Articles of War ranging from insubordination to mutiny. Twenty-eight were sentenced to terms ranging from three months to ten years." (Fold 3)

Of the 35, seven men were acquitted. Four of the men were court martialed and sentenced to three to four years hard labour. After an appeal, which focused on the poor leadership of the 1511th and the racial slurs by the MPs, a number of the sentences were reduced.

The event occurred because a small group of Afro-American soldiers had returned from Ye Olde Hob Inn where the MPs had attempted to arrest one of them, Eugene Nunn, for being improperly dressed and not having a pass. An argument ensued with the MPs on one side and the black soldiers and the locals on the other. The black soldiers returned to Adams Hall, convinced that the MPs were going to shoot them. A black officer on the base attempted to calm them down to no avail. The men armed themselves from the camp ordnance room and prepared to defend themselves when a few hours later, a large force of MPs arrived with an armoured car fitted with a machine gun. This served to compound their fears.

Ye Olde Hob Inn. (Leyland Historical Society)

*Black soldiers outside Hob Inn. (*The Battle of Bamber Bridge – *D. Rogerson)*

*Prosecution evidence – Dodge truck with bullet holes driven by one of the MPs. (*The Battle of Bamber Bridge – *D. Rogerson)*

In a report written after the event, it was the independent panel's decision that the Bamber Bridge incident had assumed serious proportions because of the readiness of both black and white servicemen to believe rumours concerning the intentions and actions of each other and because of the poor leadership on the part of the white officers who were leading the black troops.

The incident caused the authorities to review their procedures and make a number of changes with regard to Afro-American units stationed in the UK. The military archives report:

> "Not until the trouble at Bamber Bridge in June 1943, when the officers of a Negro Truck Battalion proved incapable of controlling their men, did the Commander General of the Air Force realize the extreme necessity of staffing negro units with the best, rather than the least qualified officers." (Fold 3)

In October 1943, General Devers (Commanding General of the ETO) stated clearly the US Army's policy towards racial discrimination.

*Some of the soldiers on trial. (*The Battle of Bamber Bridge – *D. Rogerson)*

> "No discrimination will be permitted against either white or colored personnel. Equal opportunities for service and recreation are the right of every American soldier regardless of branch, race, color or creed." (Fold 3)

General Eaker instituted measures to improve the running of Afro-American air force units in the UK. He attempted to purge senior ranks of inexperienced, racist officers. Yet, even after these measures, eight months later, in February 1944, there was a serious incident involving Afro-American air force personnel and white paratroopers in Leicestershire. The joint use of dance halls, pubs and ARC facilities led to altercations which resulted in the beating, stabbing and shooting of a small number of black and white US soldiers. A pitched battle with rocks, knives, bottles and clubs was narrowly averted by the combined efforts of a large number of officers.

Instead of 'educating' soldiers so that they would be able to work and spend leisure time together, more segregation was put into place across the

UK to keep the races separate, such as having separate 'black' and 'white' nights for off-duty time in local towns.

In Bamber Bridge, this sentiment was echoed by a number of publicans including the one at Ye Olde Hob Inn which instituted its own colour bar for the duration of the war: 'No White US Soldiers'.

Chapter 5

Jefferson Hall AAF 594
'A Difficult Job Well Done'

JEFFERSON HALL, Air Replacement Center Number Three, named after the third president of the United States, was the headquarters for the air force replacement centers. It was acquired by the USAAF in September 1942 and opened in October.

Jefferson Hall originally included Howard and Beatty Halls and later Duncan Hall. All three were located on adjacent sites in a village called Yarnfield, just outside Stone. At the time, Yarnfield consisted of a few farmhouses, a small country store and a pub, The Labour in Vain, which was off limits to US Army personnel. Nelson Hall, which was located at nearby Cotes Heath, was incorporated into Jefferson Hall in August 1943.

The Labour in Vain. (Yarnfield Yank)

Duncan, Beatty and Howard were sites made up of a series of H-shaped buildings enclosed by fences. In the cross bar of the Hs the common rooms were located and down the sides were small six-foot by ten-foot two person rooms with bunkbeds and windows covered by black-out curtains. In the two sides of the cross bars were utility rooms and latrines.

Each hall had a barber's shop; a dispensary which was open at all times; and a tailor's shop which offered an eight-hour service to the men for pressing their uniforms. Wool uniforms could be sent out for dry cleaning but Milton Cook recalls that they were returned smelling of aviation fuel. He also remembers that they didn't do a particularly good job, so he would often repress his own uniform when it was returned to him. The Utility Room had a large table covered with an army blanket and a tailor's shop sized electric iron had been procured so that uniforms could be steam pressed with the aid of a damp handkerchief.

Barber's Shop. (Yarnfield Yank)

Duncan Hall Dispensary. (Yarnfield Yank)

Duncan Hall also housed a chapel, a Christian League Meeting Room, and Special Service Day Rooms. Special Service also had its own separate building.

The day rooms had games such as darts, table tennis, snooker and cards. Special Service also produced a camp newsletter called the *Ardee News*. It provided equipment for the athletic field which each hall had the use of. Jefferson Hall had a softball diamond, tennis court and a pitch that could be used for American football or soccer (English football). The 70th had teams for softball, baseball, American football and soccer.

Christian League. (Yarnfield Yank)

Enlisted Men's Council. (Yarnfield Yank)

Sunday morning at Duncan Hall Chapel. (Yarnfield Yank)

Mother's Day celebrations in the Chapel. (Yarnfield Yank)

Special Service Building. (Yarnfield Yank)

Special Service. (Yarnfield Yank)

*Publications Staff. (*Yarnfield Yank*)*

ARDEE NEWS

All Highpointers Home By Xmas Says Col. Rader

Closing Dates Set

Ardee News – *newsletter produced by the Special Service. (*Yarnfield Yank*)*

*'Very Special Service'. (*Yarnfield Yank*)*

Physical Training. (Yarnfield Yank)

Casual Officers' Ball Diamond. (Fold 3)

Football Team. (Yarnfield Yank)

Jack Page. (Yarnfield Yank)

Soccer Team. (Yarnfield Yank)

Soccer Game. (Yarnfield Yank)

In June 1943, a baseball game was played on the Hough Cricket Ground in Stafford between a team from the 70th and a team made up of men from the US Army Ground Forces. Unfortunately, the 70th didn't score any runs due to the prowess of M. Collins, the pitcher for the army team. The final score was 5-0 to the Army. Over £100 was raised which went jointly to the British Red Cross and St John's fund.

Jefferson Hall was also visited by sporting celebrities such as heavyweight boxers Joe Louis and Billy Conn, rivals who visited the base separately and put on exhibition matches with sparring partners for American servicemen throughout the UK. Local resident, George Pearson, remembers one of the

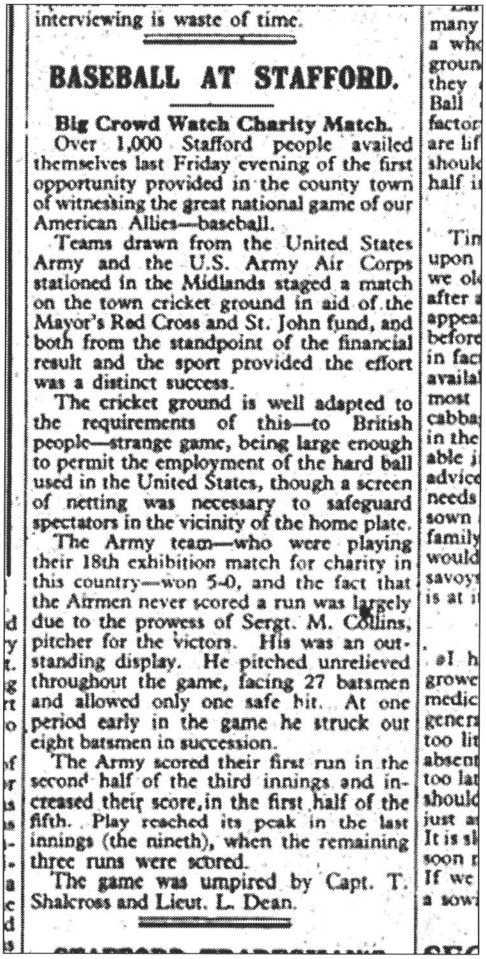

interviewing is waste of time.

BASEBALL AT STAFFORD.

Big Crowd Watch Charity Match.

Over 1,000 Stafford people availed themselves last Friday evening of the first opportunity provided in the county town of witnessing the great national game of our American Allies—baseball.

Teams drawn from the United States Army and the U.S. Army Air Corps stationed in the Midlands staged a match on the town cricket ground in aid of the Mayor's Red Cross and St. John fund, and both from the standpoint of the financial result and the sport provided the effort was a distinct success.

The cricket ground is well adapted to the requirements of this—to British people—strange game, being large enough to permit the employment of the hard ball used in the United States, though a screen of netting was necessary to safeguard spectators in the vicinity of the home plate.

The Army team—who were playing their 18th exhibition match for charity in this country—won 5-0, and the fact that the Airmen never scored a run was largely due to the prowess of Sergt. M. Collins, pitcher for the victors. His was an outstanding display. He pitched unrelieved throughout the game, facing 27 batsmen and allowed only one safe hit. At one period early in the game he struck out eight batsmen in succession.

The Army scored their first run in the second half of the third innings and increased their score in the first half of the fifth. Play reached its peak in the last innings (the nineth), when the remaining three runs were scored.

The game was umpired by Capt. T. Shalcross and Lieut. L. Dean.

Staffordshire Newsletter. *(3/7/1943)*

*Softball Team. (*Yarnfield Yank*)*

Tennis Courts. (Author's collection)

Captain Wm. J. Hapac & Major Stubbs. (Yarnfield Yank)

Joe Louis. (Yarnfield Yank)

sergeants, Joe Picararo, inviting him to meet 'The Brown Bomber'. He felt honoured to shake hands with him and in later life, when meeting people for the first time, George would often hold out his hand and say, "Shake hands with the man who shook the hand of Joe Louis."

*Billy Conn puts on his gloves with Sergeant Lee. (*Yarnfield Yank*)*

Howard Hall held the theatre, NCO club, officers' mess, casual officers' club, snack bar and hobby shop. It even had a beauty parlour with hair driers and permanent waving equipment for the use of the 120 WAC personnel on site.

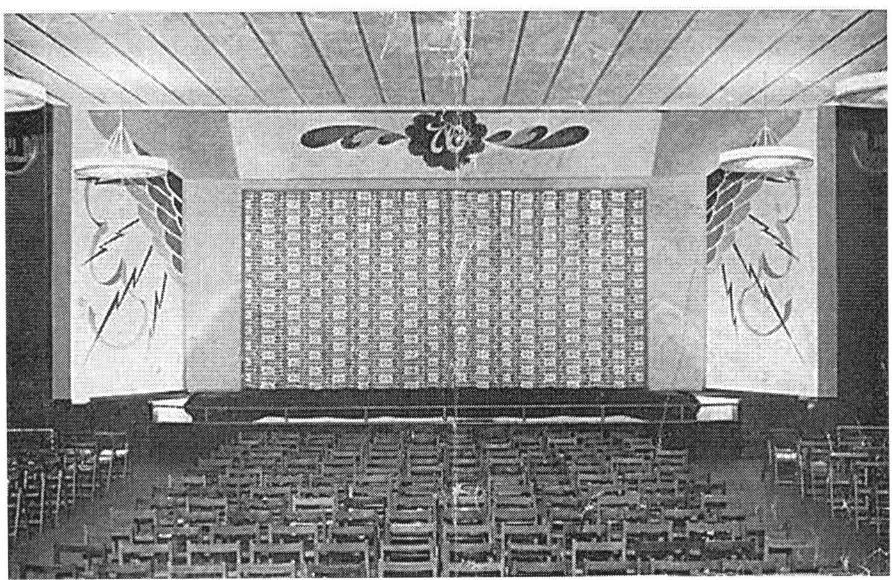

Theatre in Howard Hall. (Yarnfield Yank)

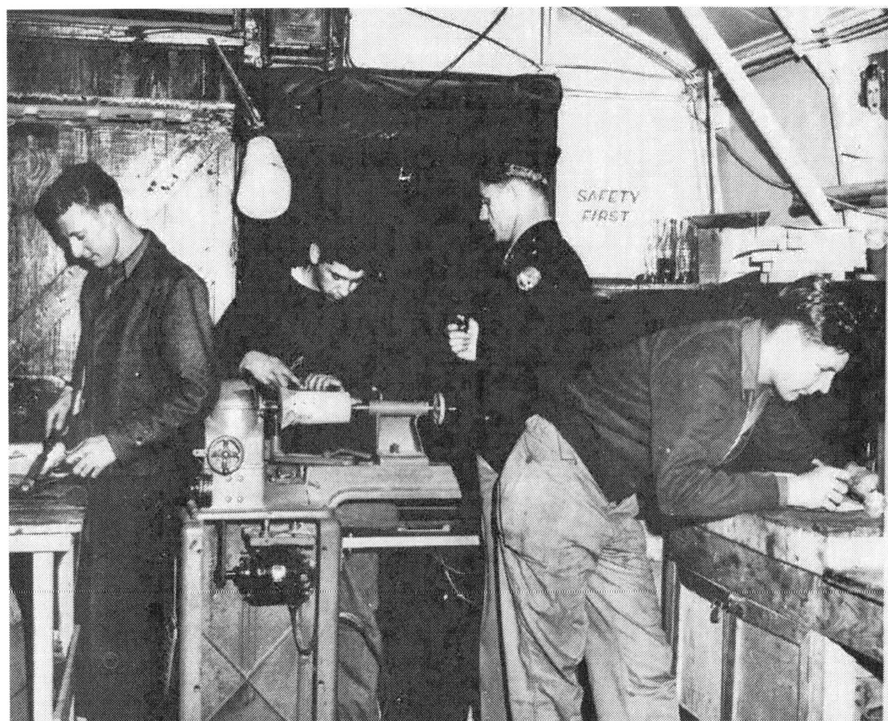

Hobby Shop. (Fold 3)

Tailor's Shop. (Yarnfield Yank)

Armed Forces Network. (Yarnfield Yank)

*Casual Officers' Club. (*Yarnfield Yank*)*

*Opening of NCO Club. (*Yarnfield Yank*)*

Officers' Snack Bar. (Fold 3)

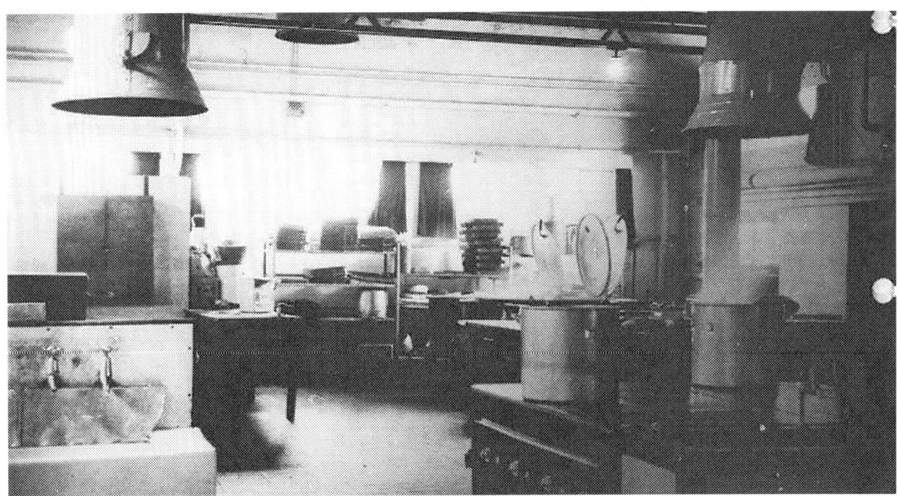

Kitchen in Howard Hall. (Fold 3)

*Officers' Mess. (*Yarnfield Yank*)*

Officers' Lounge. (Fold 3)

*Officers' Club. (*Yarnfield Yank*)*

*Home of the Permanent Staff. (*Yarnfield Yank*)*

*Rows of barracks and steam boiler building. (*That's the Way the Ball Bounces – *Milton Cook)*

*HQ offices in centre. Theatre to the left, to the right, back of officers' mess hall. (*That's the Way the Ball Bounces – *Milton Cook)*

*Permanent Staff's Officers' Mess and other buildings. (*That's the Way the Ball Bounces – *Milton Cook)*

*Permanent Officers' Mess and back of mess hall kitchen. (*That's the Way the Ball Bounces – *Milton Cook)*

*Chow Formation. (*Yarnfield Yank*)*

*Chow Line. (*Yarnfield Yank*)*

Casual Officers' Dining Room. (Fold 3)

The WACs were billeted between the guardhouse and the theatre in a long rectangular building which was originally the permanent officers' quarters. Most of the WACs were employed in processing paperwork for air force personnel arriving from and returning to the US. A small number worked in the PX. WAC, Angeline Frank, remembers working at Nelson Hall (where she was transported from Howard Hall each day) on book-keeping and tailoring. MP, Milton Cook, remembers that the WACs were the only unit billeted in Jefferson Hall, that routinely marched as a company singing songs such as, *Be kind to your web-footed friends for a duck may be somebody's mother.* WACs were not the only females on the post. A group of Red Cross girls ran an aeroclub on site as well as doughnut and coffee snack bars.

WACs in the library at Howard Hall. (Fold 3)

WACs at work. (Yarnfield Yank)

Red Cross Fashion Show. (Yarnfield Yank)

Red Cross Club. (Fold 3)

PX. (Fold 3)

Post Exchange. (Yarnfield Yank)

The well-stocked PX at Jefferson Hall used a ration-card system. Each week the men were allowed to purchase seven packets of cigarettes or 21 cigars and two boxes of matches. Those that didn't smoke gave their allocations to someone who did. The servicemen were also entitled to 6oz of sweets and a packet of gum or Life-savers per week. Razor blades and soap could also be bought at the PX. Seven pints of beer could be purchased per week from the PX, however most of the men preferred to buy their beer from the pubs in the local towns.

The PX also sold fine china like Royal Doulton, Spode and Wedgewood. The authorities thought that having souvenirs to buy on base to send home would prevent the men from 'splashing the cash' around the local towns where it might cause resentment from their British counterparts. The PX was also the place where war bonds could be bought. The cost was deducted from the men's wages and the bonds were sent to family back home.

In the central structure of Howard Hall there was a station theatre, enlisted men's lounge, administration offices and mess facilities. In the two wings were the enlisted men's and casual officers' mess halls. The theatre showed recent Hollywood releases three times a day for two consecutive days so that all those on duty would have a chance to see the films. Milton Cook remembers watching Danny Kaye in *Up in Arms* every night that he wasn't on duty. The seating in the theatre consisted of wooden chairs that could be folded to create space for dances. The 70th had its own dance band called *The Kansas City Six and Chris*, which would sometimes play in the theatre hall for dances. The theatre was also the venue for USO shows about once a month. Bob Hope and his troupe performed there in the early part of 1943.

The Kansas City Six and Chris. (Yarnfield Yank)

The food served in the mess halls at the 70th was good compared with what the local residents were eating at the time. Milton Cook recalls that breakfast was usually grapefruit or other tinned fruit followed by SOS (stuff on a shingle) which was ground beef in gravy on toast – a good way to use up stale bread. Cook remembers wartime bread in the UK as being greyish and coarse in texture. For the main meal, there would be powdered eggs, dehydrated potatoes, carrots and onions. Fish was eaten on Fridays. On Thanksgiving Day and Christmas Day there would be a roast turkey with mashed potato, tinned sweet potatoes and gravy.

On the office side of the hallway in Howard Hall was the enlisted men's lounge. A visitor's book was kept there which was signed by soldiers who spent time there. Unusually, one officer had his name signed in the book – Clark Gable, hometown Hollywood, California. Unfortunately, later someone ripped the page out of the book to keep as a souvenir.

*Chief Projectionist. (*Yarnfield Yank*)*

Jefferson Hall also had a post office where casuals would sort the mail and forward it to the correct unit. Casuals were rarely at the depot long enough to receive mail themselves. Permanent staff often received packages from home. Cook remembers receiving home-made cookies wrapped in waxed paper and packed in popped corn. The popcorn would still be edible by the time it arrived. Cook requested that his mother sent corn kernels so that he could 'pop' them with butter in a mess tin on a hot plate in the mess hall.

Occasionally Cook's fellow MP, Collins, received fresh oranges from the States. His uncle was an engineer who worked in a citrus packing plant with a machine that washed and waxed fruit. The uncle would often send his nephew a box of fruit as an experiment to see how the oranges survived the journey.

Army Post Office. (Yarnfield Yank)

Directory Section, Army Post Office. (Fold 3)

Unit Distribution, Army Post Office. (Fold 3)

Thursdays in Jefferson Hall was 'gas mask day'. Gas masks were to be carried at all times on this day as personnel from the Chemical Warfare Section, known as 'stinkers', would often drive around the post lobbing CS-2 tear gas grenades to see how quickly the men could 'mask up'. Cook found this quite disruptive to the normal 'repple-depple' activities.

*Ordnance and Chemical Warfare Section. (*Yarnfield Yank*)*

*'The Stinkers'. (*Yarnfield Yank*)*

Jefferson Hall was subject to a number of official inspections. Early in 1944, Cook was on duty at the gate to Duncan Hall, when a black staff car arrived from the direction of Stone. It had two pennants, a Stars and Stripes on one side and on the other, a red flag with four white stars – which signified that a General was being driven in the car.

The car didn't slow down as it neared the entrance and it was obvious that it wasn't going to stop, so Cook snapped to attention and saluted. He received three salutes back from the rear of the car. In the centre was Major General Cal A. Spaatz, the Commander of the US Strategic Air Forces (USSTAF) in the ETO (the 70th was part of his command as it processed Air Force personnel in the ETO). To his left, was Lieutenant General Ira E. Eaker, who at the time was commander of the Mediterranean Allied Air Forces (MAAF) in the MTO (Mediterranean Theater of Operations).

Gas Chamber. (Fold 3)

The visit was billed as an inspection tour but Cook wondered if it was more of a 'social call' to Colonel Radar as it was unusual for such high-ranking officers to inspect a base unless there was a specific issue to deal with. Cook also found it strange that Eaker was involved in the inspection party as, at the time, he did not have an executive position in the ETO.

Colonel Radar meets the Generals. (Yarnfield Yank)

Colonel Radar, General Spaatz and General Doolittle. (Yarnfield Yank)

*Air Inspector and Staff. (*Yarnfield Yank*)*

On another occasion, Jefferson Hall was inspected by Lieutenant Colonel Frederick C. Robert Jr who found that:

> "Discipline is of a slightly more strict nature than encountered on Tactical Air Force installations." (Fold 3)

Although he also noticed:

> "Saluting is stressed but casual offices appear to pay little heed." (Fold 3)

Of Colonel Radar, the CO, he stated:

> "He is very energetic in the performance of his duties. He is conscientious and appears to have planned foremost on any job that may be required of him in the performance of his mission as Depot Commander. I would consider him an excellent officer." (Fold 3)

Of the base as a whole, he concluded:

> "This depot is operated in a very systematic manner and - - - is to be complimented on a difficult job well done." (Fold 3)

Chapter 6

1257th MP Battalion. Working Side by Side

TO KEEP the order both on the post and in the nearby towns, the 1257th MP Battalion was attached to the 12th RCD at Jefferson Hall. The unit, commanded by Captain Bishop, arrived on the post in August 1943. One of the MPs, Milton Cook, remembers that Captain Bishop obtained leather Sam Brown pistol belts for the whole company. The rumour was that he did this because he wanted to wear one himself. Cook remembers that he regularly socialised with the local gentry in the area and often joined them on hunts on their estates.

Bill Amrhein. (That's the Way the Ball Bounces – *Milton Cook)*

One of the members of the 1257th, Bill Amrhein, had an interesting history. He had been born in Germany and had actually served in the Hitler Youth. His uncle, who was living in America, sponsored him so that he was able to emigrate to the USA, however, he was still a German citizen when he was inducted into the US Army. In the Spring of 1944, US Congress law allowed foreign-born servicemen and women to apply for US citizenship. Amrhein travelled from Stone to Birmingham, to take the oath of citizenship. At the end of the war, he signed up for a further three-year stint and became part of the Army of

Occupation in Germany because he could speak fluent German. Following this, he returned to his homeland as a US citizen.

Jefferson Hall had a large guardhouse with capacity for 30 men. It also served as a headquarters for the MP Battalion. The whole site at Jefferson Hall was enclosed by a fence with two large swinging vehicle gates which were closed and latched each evening. There was also a small gate for pedestrians, which was sometimes closed at night. Duncan Hall had two gates facing the Yarnfield Road. During the day, the west gate was the entrance to the camp and the east gate, the exit. Both were closed in the evening. During the day, the three station gates were manned by two MPs each. Two of the gates and the guardhouse were manned around the clock by members of the 1257th.

Duncan Hall, Entrance Number 2. (That's the Way the Ball Bounces – *Milton Cook)*

Snowstorm at entrance. (Yarnfield Yank)

Milton Cook on duty. (That's the Way the Ball Bounces – *Milton Cook*)

Milton Cook on duty. (That's the Way the Ball Bounces – *Milton Cook)*

MPs on duty. (That's the Way the Ball Bounces – *Milton Cook)*

Milton Cook. (That's the Way the Ball Bounces – *Milton Cook)*

Cook, Foiles and Collins at the rear of MP barracks and common room. (That's the Way the Ball Bounces – *Milton Cook)*

Cook, Saloka and Andriko in front of MP barracks. (That's the Way the Ball Bounces – *Milton Cook)*

MP, John Brooks. (Nick Brooks)

MPs at Retreat, John Brooks in the middle. (Nick Brooks)

Group of MPs, John Brooks, 3rd Left. (Nick Brooks)

John Brooks with colleague on Harley Davidsons. (Nick Brooks)

An MP would also be on point duty from early in the morning until the last man was back on the post. Point duty involved standing in the centre of the road that led from Yarnfield Road to the depot. One of the MP's duties would be to check that the vehicles from the post were driving on the correct side of the road. This was a mistake that was frequently made. Casual, Richard Butler, writes in a V-mail back home:

> "- - - this driving down the left side of the street has me worried." (*P-38 Odyssey* – Dick Butler)

Richard Butler and his brother, Heber, managed to procure bikes while they were at Jefferson Hall to cycle to Stone and Stafford. At the end of his bike ride, Richard records in his journal:

> "- - - these rolling hills all over that distance turns out to be quite a ways. Frankly, I'm ready for bed." (*P-38 Odyssey* – Dick Butler)

In a V-mail he comments:

> "We stopped at a tea shop on the way back. I really went in for a drink of water, but we ordered chocolate and sandwiches - - - People think you're crazy if you drink anything but tea. She even tried to talk me out of it - - - I don't dare ask for a drink of milk for fear they'll recommend me for a discharge." (*P-38 Odyssey* – Dick Butler)

In his journal he notes:

> "People around here sure go for their tea. War or no war, if they want some tea, they close up shop and proceed to get a cup. If you don't drink tea or beer, you're barmy." (*P-38 Odyssey* – Dick Butler)

WAC, Beulah Johnson, also enjoyed cycling around Yarnfield. She wrote to her family that she had been spending most of her time:

> "On top of that bicycle going down country lanes and 'flying down hills'." (Beulah Johnson's letters, Laura Ellis Lai)

She continues:

> "It has been so comfortable I have done the unforgivable in the army – ridden along with my blouse [jacket] unbuttoned and my hat off so that the wind can blow thru my hair. I was just lucky no MPs came along." (Beulah Johnson's letters, Laura Ellis Lai)

(Beulah's colleague from the base had been stopped by the MPs for this offence.) However she goes on to comment that:

> "I still would rather have a horse, because it doesn't need me to balance it - - - I have only had the one [spill] since I have been riding and that was - - - when I first began. It is surprising what cinders can do when you scrape a leg in them." (Beulah Johnson's letters, Laura Ellis Lai)

Later, one of the permanent NCOs on the post set up a bike rental business at Jefferson Hall, so that bikes could be rented out to casual GIs on a pass. One evening, two GIs, who were riding on a tandem towards the post, came flying past the MP on point duty. Just before they crashed headlong into a tree, one was heard to yell, "This is more fun than a barrel of monkeys." They were the last words either would hear or say. The next day, the sergeant was out of the bike rental business.

Another death of a man from the 70th on the road was reported in the *Staffordshire Sentinel* on 29 February 1944. Sergeant Benjamin Vaccaro received fatal injuries when he was hit by a civilian lorry driven by Eric Harrison in November 1943. Harrison's defence was that Vaccaro had stepped off the footpath in front of the lorry.

Bicycle Repair. (Yarnfield Yank)

Milton Cook's first assigned duty as an MP at the barracks, was to man the

~~SECRET~~

HEADQUARTERS
70TH REPLACEMENT DEPOT (AAF)
Office of the Provost Marshal
APO 652

VIOLATIONS FROM 1 JAN 45, TO AND INCLUDING 31 JAN 45

VIOLATIONS	153rd Co HOWARD	154th Co DUNCAN	155th Co	156th Co BEATTY	158th Co BEATTY	162nd Co NELSON	163rd Co NELSON	164th Co	70th RD (AAF)	93rd Sta Comp Sq RD	WAC Det	Hq & Hq 133rd Bn	Med Det	Pos Det
Pass Violations	9	24		26	11					1	1			
Uniform Violations		5		3										
Insubordination														
Bicycle Violations														
A W O L	5	11		4	2					1				1
Off Limits		2		1										
Assault														
Vehicle		1							1					
Drunk and/or Disorderly		2		1			1							
Indecent Conduct														
Handkerchief Violations														
Miscellaneous	1	4			2									
TOTAL	15	49		35	15		1		1	2	1			1

Violations Form. (Fold 3)

gates of Howard and Duncan Halls. The job required him to check documents of vehicles and log them in and out of the depot. Colonel Radar, who drove a distinctive sporty Jaguar with amber headlights was never stopped at the gates to show his pass.

MPs also checked the passes of pedestrians entering and exiting the base. Passes for casual personnel were restricted to up to six hours between the hours of 1600 and 2400. Civilian buses were available to take personnel with passes into the nearby towns and pick them up at the end of the evening. When the MPs drew patrol duty, they were often picked up and dropped off in jeeps. Cook remembers that some jeeps had plexiglass and plywood sides and doors to make them warmer.

The village of Yarnfield was so small that it didn't require MP patrols, however it was necessary for MPs to police Mill Meece, the small village where Nelson Hall and ROF Swynnerton were located because of the casual airmen billeted at Nelson Hall. Eccleshall was also patrolled by MPs. Although Eccleshall was a small village with just two intersecting main streets, it was popular with the casual GIs from Jefferson Hall as it was the location of the halls which housed the female munition workers for ROF Swynnerton. Milton Cook recalls that it was often difficult to persuade GIs on passes in Eccleshall to return to base at the end of the evening.

Above: Souvenir mug from the Fitzherbert Arms in Swynnerton. (Laura Ellis Lai)
Below: Other items of Staffordshire Pottery collected by Beulah Johnson. (Laura Ellis Lai)

The MPs became friendly with Eileen Hurlstone who ran the tobacco shop in Eccleshall. She would occasionally send gifts of Staffordshire China to their parents. Staffordshire China was popular with the men and women of the 70th. Some members like Beulah Johnson would try and collect whole tea sets, piece by piece. She preferred to go to Mintons to build up her set. In return, Cook's parents sent linen handkerchiefs which were difficult to obtain in the UK because of clothes rationing. They would wash the handkerchiefs first so that they could be classified as 'used' to avoid paying custom duty.

Beulah Johnson.

The town of Stone was also patrolled by the MPs of the 1257th. There was a pub located on the road that ran from Yarnfield Road and many of the GIs never got past the first pub, although there were others in the town. Stone also had a Donut Dugout at St Joseph's Hall that supplied coffee and doughnuts to the GIs.

In a letter to her family, Beulah Johnson mentions cycling to the Donut Dugout to play ping-pong. She comments:

> "It is quieter there than at our club [on the base] - - - and there are not really as many people around." (Beulah Johnson's letters, Laura Ellis Lai)

The catholic church also held dances for servicemen and local girls. Other attractions in Stone were the fish and chip shop and the Stone Brewery. Stone Baggage, where the men's luggage was stored while awaiting transport to the replacement depot, was located at the top

Beulah Johnson.

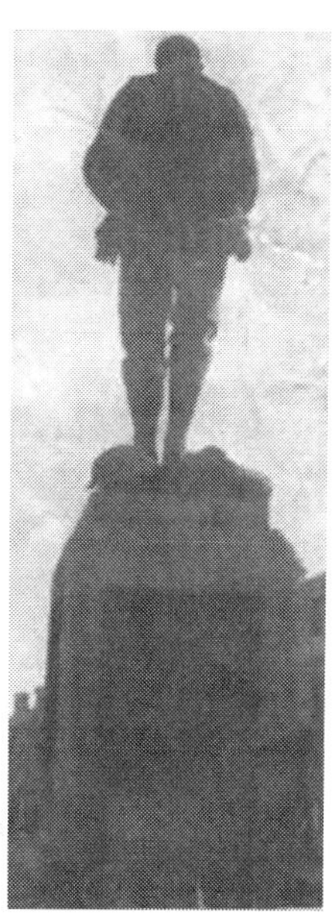

War Memorial in High Street, Stone. (Yarnfield Yank)

Building in Stone formerly known as St Joseph's that was used by the Red Cross as a Donut Dugout. (M. Collins)

of the main street by the railway station.

On 13 July 1944, the *Staffordshire Sentinel* reports on the case of a 'helplessly drunk' British citizen who was 'helped' into an MP's jeep in Stone and transported to the police station. On another occasion the newspaper reports on three American airmen from the 70th who crashed into a pigsty outside Crossfield House because they were the worse for drink. Two of the men ran off and were later arrested by the MPs. Fortunately, the resident managed to rescue several of his pigs.

Inside the Red Cross Club in Stone. (Yarnfield Yank)

Another place that the MPs from Jefferson Hall patrolled was the somewhat larger town of Stafford which produced an information booklet for the US Armed Forces as a guide for its American visitors. The pubs there closed at 10.00pm, so the MPs had little to do all evening until this time when they would check all the social clubs and pubs for stragglers.

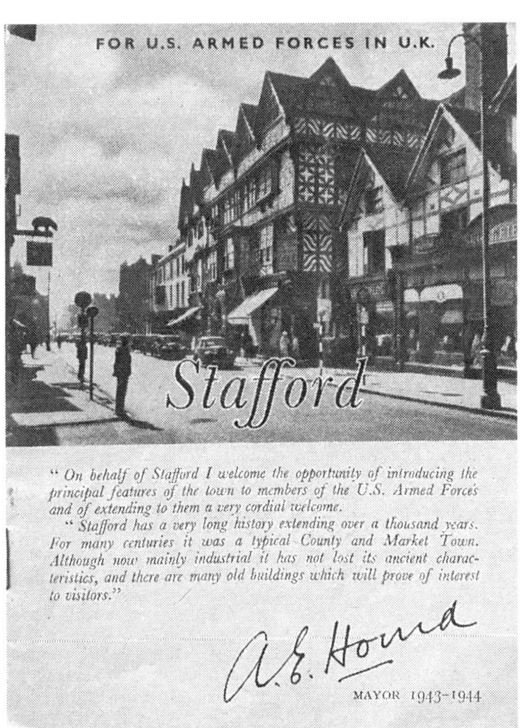

Booklet produced for the US Armed Forces. (Author's collection)

There were two other towns in the area that GIs from Jefferson Hall, would

Red Cross Club in Hanley. (Fold 3)

visit on passes. One was Hanley where there was an ARC club staffed by local residents where men could have bed and breakfast for 2/6 (12½p). The other town was Stoke-on-Trent which had two cinemas.

One man in the MP Battalion was never given a patrol duty. He was the shortest man in the company and only just made the minimum height requirement for being an MP. He was close to 40 years old and it was thought that he would be unable to carry out regular patrol duties so his role was to police the enlisted men's snack bar and lounge where the strongest drinks available were coffee and coke.

The MPs themselves were entitled to passes, leaves and furloughs. Milton Cook remembers visiting Birmingham and also going to London on a two

Enlisted Men's Snack Bar. (Fold 3)

day pass. In his two and a half years' service overseas, he had only one short furlough. He and two of his colleagues planned to spend it in Blackpool. When they arrived at the guardhouse to procure transport to Stone, they learnt that there had been a 'shut down' and all passes and vehicle traffic had been suspended. MPs had set up road blocks to intercept errant truck drivers. Fortunately, MPs were exempt from the travel ban so their furlough could go ahead.

MPs off duty. (That's the Way the Ball Bounces – *Milton Cook)*

*MPs off duty (*That's the Way the Ball Bounces – *Milton Cook)*

Issued 11 Nov 1943 by [illegible]
(Da.) (Mo.) (Yr.) (Signature of Issuing Officer)

[illegible]
(Name) (Grade) (Branch)

Loss of this card will be reported immediately to the C.O. of the individual named hereon.

The finder of a lost card will please return it to Headquarters, SOS, ETOUSA, APO 871, U.S. Army.

This card is void if altered in any manner, unless such alterations are initialed by the responsible officer.

Identification Card No. **E** 043320

(S.7617)

ENLISTED MAN'S IDENTIFICATION CARD
European Theater of Operations, U.S. Army

This is to identify MILTON E. COOK

whose description and signature appear hereon, as a member of the United States armed forces, serving in the European Theater of Operations.

Grade Pvt. Asn. 3956[illegible] Race White

Home address Adelanto, California

Birthplace [illegible]

Birthdate [illegible] Sept 192[illegible] 5 11
(Da.) (Mo.) (Yr.) Height ft. ins.

Weight 166 lbs. (11 stones 12 lbs.)

Color hair brown Color eyes blue Complexion medium

Scars or distinguishing marks

Milton E. Cook
(Signature of soldier)

*Milton Cook's Pass (*That's the Way the Ball Bounces – *Milton Cook)*

*Cook, Foiles and Strehlaw on furlough in Blackpool. (*That's the Way the Ball Bounces – *Milton Cook)*

The men first caught a train to Bolton from Stone and then it was necessary to wait for the train to Blackpool. Ironically, while awaiting the train, their papers were inspected by local MPs who were looking for AWOL GIs. The stay in Blackpool was enjoyed by the three men, particularly as it was the only time that they had a real bed with sheets for the duration that they were in the UK. At the end of the war a large number of GIs, including Cook, were awarded $175 in leave bonds to compensate for the furloughs that they had been entitled to, but had been unable to take.

*On furlough in Blackpool. (*That's the Way the Ball Bounces – *Milton Cook)*

In his duties as MP, it was often necessary for Cook to travel across the country to pick up servicemen that had gone AWOL. He regularly travelled to air bases in East Anglia and into London. On the way to Chorley to pick up a prisoner charged with being AWOL, he remembers seeing a large number of people lining the side of the roads. He was halted by a British policeman and as he waited, he saw a black Rolls Royce with a liveried driver advancing slowly along the street. In the rear of the car sat King George and Queen Elizabeth.

In March 1944, Cook had his best assignment, which was to accompany a sergeant on a five-day trip to collect a serviceman who had gone AWOL in France. Cook and the Sergeant flew on the *Froggy Bottom Express*, the designated aircraft for the 70th RD, from Seighford Airfield.

*Froggy Bottom Express. (*Yarnfield Yank*)*

The prisoner was held at Château Rothschild where Cook remembers eating a breakfast of fried eggs, bacon, toast, coffee and fresh grapefruit served by German POWs. He noticed that the segments of grapefruit had been cut the wrong way and he wondered if the Germans had done it on purpose to make it difficult to eat. During his stay at the Château, Cook had time for sight-seeing in Paris. He managed to see the Eiffel Tower (which was closed to the public), Notre Dame, the Arc de Triomphe and the Champs Elysee.

*Château Rothschild – in the foreground the mess tent is erected on the entrance terrace. The chimney pipe from the mess tent stoves runs up the outside of the château walls. (*Yarnfield Yank*)*

*'At Ease' – Château Rothschild Latrine. (*That's the Way the Ball Bounces – *Milton Cook)*

At the end of August 1944, when Cook was back in England, there was a severe fuel shortage on the Continent which was hampering the flow of supplies to the front lines. A command decision was made to airlift as much fuel and supplies into the Continent from the UK as possible. This produced a critical need of air transport crews. Unfortunately, many of the air transport casuals from Jefferson Hall had been given passes before the need was realised. Cook was given the job of checking all the pubs in Stone to search for air transport crew who could help in the crisis. Unfortunately, he was unable to find even one person. Nevertheless, the necessary fuel was delivered to the Continent and the supply chain was restored.

Another duty carried out by MPs at Jefferson Hall, was the guarding of USAAF plane crashes within a designated area of the Midlands. This duty would often involve standing in a cold damp field for several hours until the air force recovery team arrived. For this duty, the men learnt to wear their field jackets and fatigue trousers underneath their wool coats and trousers. They were also issued with grey woollen RAF scarves. The men wrote home to their mothers to knit them jumpers and sleeveless tops which they would wear under their uniform.

One P-38 Lightning that Cook was responsible for guarding, had a wheels-up crash landing. Fortunately, the only damage was to the propellers that were bent. Once the recovery team had arrived, it was necessary to remove the outer sections of the wings in order to move it by truck along the narrow country roads.

Cook was also asked to stand guard over a P-47 Thunderbolt which had crash landed in similar circumstances. While waiting, it was necessary to ensure that the steady stream of families from the nearby houses did not touch anything. Among the onlookers, Cook noticed a heavily made-up lady. Later he was relieved by another MP but was puzzled when that MP did not return to base when he in turn was relieved. The MP returned eight hours later, having spent the night with the lady that Cook noticed.

Cook also remembers seeing a bomber plane crash and burn just north of Beatty Hall after it had just buzzed the replacement depot. In the Summer of 1944, the same thing nearly happened when the depot was buzzed by a P-47 Thunderbolt which had dived steeply then pulled up about five feet from the ground. The whole of the 1257th witnessed this event as they had just had a battalion photo taken. To ensure that all of the 1257th were in the photo

1257th MP Battalion. (Yarnfield Yank)

necessitated asking other servicemen to temporarily cover MP duties on the gates and guardhouse.

On another occasion, a German aircraft had crashed after the local Home Guard Unit had shot at it. The men of the Home Guard were heard boasting about their shooting skills in the Beehive pub in Eccleshall. It was later found that the plane had been stolen from the Luftwaffe by three Polish servicemen who had flown it to the UK. It had crash landed because it had run out of fuel. An inspection showed that there were no bullet holes to suggest that the Home Guard had hit their target.

While stationed at Jefferson Hall, the MP Battalion were invited to take part in a number of parades in the local towns, partly because they looked so smart. They had a number of strategies for looking debonair. One was to tie two condoms together to make a garter so that the bottom of their trousers would blouse out.

In September 1944, the 1257th were invited to march in the Battle of Britain Parade in Eccleshall. The parade finished at St Michael's Church, where, in his address to the troops, the Reverend Salt took the opportunity to single out the American soldiers and chastise them for 'blemishing' English women in general and the ladies of the village in particular. In 1945, the Battle of Britain Parade was longer with more units involved. Cook remembers that it ended in a field of damp grass where the men got colder and colder as they stood to attention.

Personnel from the 70th Replacement Depot also took part in the Wings for Victory Parade in Stone in May 1944. In his address at the end, Sir Ralph Wedgewood emphasised the importance of the Battle of Britain:

> "- - - making this country supreme in the air as it was on the sea." (*Staffordshire Newsletter* 15/5/1944)

He included the American servicemen present by qualifying the above remark.

> "When he said this country, he associated in that, our cousins across the Atlantic, with whom he wished to share that supremacy. He believed that in the air there were great opportunities for us to share, by working side by side." (*Staffordshire Newsletter* 15/5/1944)

Among the officers taking the salute for the parade was Colonel Harvey H. Holland of the United States Army Air Force. The saluting base was flanked by the Stars and Stripes and the Union Jack. The activities during the Wings for Victory Week raised over £80,000 to purchase four Mosquito aircraft for the RAF.

Eccleshall Battle of Britain Day Parade. (That's the Way the Ball Bounces – *Milton Cook)*

Parade in Stafford. (Yarnfield Yank)

Military Police. (Yarnfield Yank)

Colonel Radar reviews 659th AAF band and MPs. (Yarnfield Yank)

Chapter 7

70th Replacement Depot et al

Bruche Hall

Bruche Hall, located in Warrington, was constructed during the early part of the war to provide accommodation for workers at ROF Risley. It was never used to house the munition workers and in 1942 it was acquired by the USAAF to use as a transit camp for nearby RAF Burtonwood (AAF 590) Aircraft Maintenance Depot.

The site had accommodation for around 2,000 servicemen, living in H-block buildings similar to the buildings at Yarnfield. There were ablutions, mess facilities and a central hall often used as a dance hall. As such, it was ideal to use as part of the replacement depot system.

Bruche Hall. (Gary Lea)

As mentioned in Chapter 1, Bruche Hall was not released to the replacement system in June 1943 as requested, but there is evidence to suggest that it was used at peak times. As its photograph is included in the original *Yarnfield Yank*, we can be certain that it was incorporated into the 70th at some point.

*Bruche Hall. (*Yarnfield Yank*)*

Bruche Hall, 1942. (Ted Wurm)

Bruche Hall, 1942. (Ted Wurm)

Bruche Hall. (Gary Lea)

Bruche Hall, 1942. (Ted Wurm)

Bruche Hall, 1942. Theatre from Officers' Quarters. (Ted Wurm)

Bruche Hall. (Ted Wurm)

B-24 coming in over Bruche Hall. (Gary Lea)

Meaford Hall

Other buildings in the vicinity of Stone were used by the US forces. Meaford Hall, a seventeenth-century country house on the outskirts of Stone, was occupied by the 35th Evacuation Hospital for a few months in 1944. The hall had previously been sold by the family who owned it in 1943 and, during the war, it was also used by the pupils of Alleyne's Grammar School which was situated in Uttoxeter.

The 6th US Convalescent Hospital made arrangements for the 35th to be billeted in the hall and in the village of Meaford. Personnel from the 35th arrived in Stone by overnight train from the port of Gourock, Scotland, arriving at 0300 hours on 19 February 1944. The hall became the headquarters of the 35th while it was stationed in England.

The personnel soon found that staying in a historic house was not particularly comfortable. The hall was distinctly draughty and, although it had more than 20 fireplaces, few could be used because of coal rationing. Bathing and laundry facilities were also sparse with one tap shared between 200 men.

Meaford Hall, 1944 while occupied by 35th Evacuation Hospital. (Stuart Smith – World War II Photos)

During their time in England, the personnel of the 35th carried out training and orientation for their role as an evacuation hospital on the Continent. There was also time for the men to take part in extra-curricular activities such as softball. The 35th had a softball team that was undefeated in England.

The 35th was alerted for movement across the English Channel on 3 May 1944, but did not move from Meaford until 18 June when it travelled to the marshalling area at Southampton. From there, the advance party boarded a ship to Omaha Beach, Normandy, arriving on 19 June. Unfortunately, poor weather meant that the unit was unable to dock for five days. During this time the area received nightly bombardments. After arriving in France, the unit set up a hospital in Carentan. In August, it began its journey through France, Luxembourg and then Germany, following the combat units and carrying out its role as an evacuation hospital.

Meaford Hall through window, 1944 while occupied by 35th Evacuation Hospital. (Stuart Smith – World War II Photos)

Keele Hall AAF 536

Another camp in the locality of Stone used as part of the 70th replacement depot was Keele Park Estate (now part of Keele University) near Newcastle-under-Lyme. A detachment of the 18th Replacement Control Depot were billeted there at one point and it was also used to billet 2096 QM Trucking Company (Aviation) which was probably an Afro-American unit (see appendix 4 for complete list of units billeted at Keele).

Keele Hall had been requisitioned in 1939 by the military for wartime use. At the time, the landowner was living in Wiltshire. The hall was occupied by servicemen as was part of the Clock House, as well as a number of temporary buildings which were erected to house the troops in the grounds. At the beginning of the war, several British units used the camp, including forces evacuated from Dunkirk.

A number of US units were billeted temporarily at Keele throughout the war. The Command Post of the US 83rd Infantry Division was stationed at Keele Hall from 19 April to 14 June 1944. While billeted there, the troops were trained at locations across Wales and Shropshire before moving to a base near Stonehenge ready to be shipped to Normandy.

Jeff Goodwin, who had been evacuated to Keele from London at the beginning of the war, has some memories of the Americans based there. Jeff was first fostered, and later adopted by John Goodwin, who was the agent for Keele Estate, and his wife, Mary. John worked from offices in the Clock House so he and Jeff were given official passes to get on and off the site through one of the two sentry positions along the road leading from the village to the camp.

Walking through the camp, Jeff remembers being given armfuls of candy from the GIs. He also remembers seeing tanks, ordnance and other military vehicles parked under the trees on either side of the drive which would give them a degree of camouflage. On one occasion, Jeff and his stepfather were given a ride in one of the tanks that flattened a number of trees. Jeff also recalls seeing General Patton (wearing his signature pearl-handled pistol) addressing the troops outside the Clock House on his visit to the area.

The sentries became used to Jeff walking through the camp to meet his stepfather in the Clock House and would usually wave him into the grounds without checking his pass. There was one instance when he forgot his pass and unfortunately came face to face with an unfamiliar sentry, who marched him to the Clock House to check his identity with John Goodwin. The sentry's stern expression soon changed to mirth when his stepfather vouched for him.

John Goodwin would invite the American servicemen who were interested to join him on shooting and fishing expeditions on the estate. The family often entertained American officers to eat at their house and Mary decided to write to General Eisenhower to tell him how charming and polite

Aerial photograph of the Keele Estate, Staffordshire, 11 August 1945, by No. 541 Squadron RAF. GB172 UGSD61 Special Collections and Archives, Keele University Library.

the American soldiers were. Surprisingly, the general replied to her letter, thanking them for their hospitality towards the US servicemen. On 25 June, the 83rd were shipped to Normandy where they took part in the push across France to Germany.

After the war, an inscription etched by Clyde Applegate, a US soldier from Fort Smith, Arkansas, was found on the gates to Keele Hall. Sadly, it was found that although Quinton Clyde Applegate had survived combat duty with the 83rd, he had died in 1948 at the age of 27 after an illness.

After the war, the base was converted into a camp for refugees and later, the military buildings that had been constructed on the site, were used to house students from Keele University.

Colonel Stark and staff officers on lawn at Keele Hall. (Photo courtesy of Brampton Museum, Newcastle-under-Lyme Borough Council)

John Goodwin, US Officer and Courtney Campbell (local dentist). Shooting party on Keele Estate. (Jeff Goodwin)

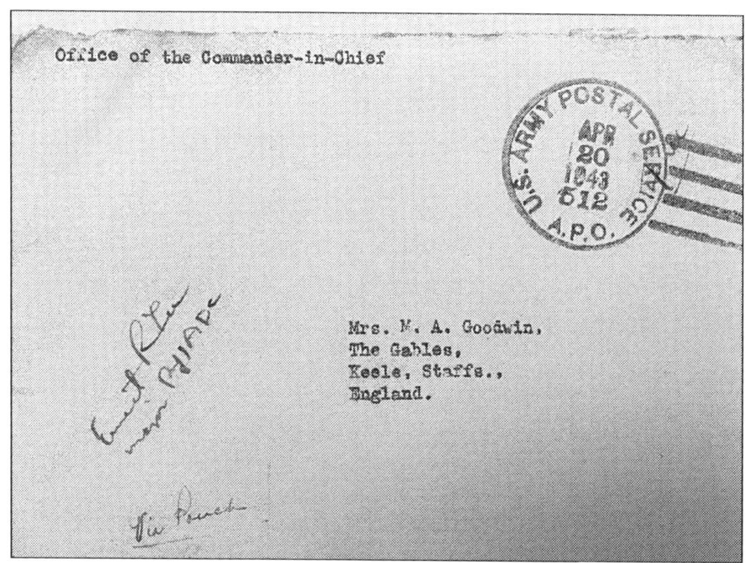

Office of the Commander-in-Chief

U.S. ARMY POSTAL SERVICE
APR
20
1943
512
A.P.O.

Mrs. M. A. Goodwin,
The Gables,
Keele, Staffs.,
England.

Letter received by Mary Goodwin from General Eisenhower. (Jeff Goodwin)

Mrs. M. A. Goodwin,
The Gables,
Keele, Staffs.,
England.

ALLIED FORCE HEADQUARTERS
Office of the Commander-in-Chief

19 April, 1943.

Dear Mrs. Goodwin:

I greatly appreciate the patriotic spirit which prompts you to write your note of April 8th.

You have expressed most effectively the sense of comradeship that prevails between the British and Americans in this Allied Command.

Thank you for writing to me.

Sincerely,

Dwight D Eisenhower

Mrs. M. A. Goodwin
The Gables
Keele, Staffs.,
England.

Letter received by Mary Goodwin from General Eisenhower. (Jeff Goodwin)

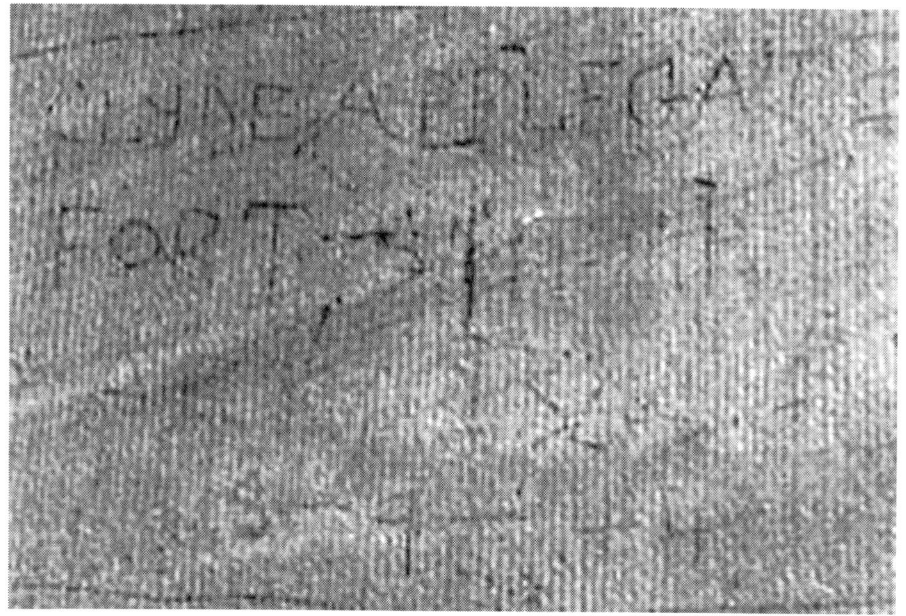

Inscription on Keele Hall gate post. (Keele University Library)

Wartime buildings used post-war as part of Keele University Campus. (Keele University Library)

Students in front of wartime constructions, post-war. (Keele University Library)

Rest Homes – 70th RD

Soon after the 12th RCD was established in the UK, the authorities decided that 'rest homes' were needed by the USAAF to give flyers the much needed rest and recuperation (R and R) for a short period, so that the air crew were able to continue functioning in the most efficient way. As the military archives report:

> "It became very apparent in the latter part of 1942 that the combat man would need from time to time, during their operational tour, a place to go for complete relaxation. Our men, unlike the British fliers, could not spend their leaves at home, so a new form of hospitality was thrown open to members of the Eighth and Ninth Air Forces. The officers and enlisted men, as a result of nervous strain imposed on them by high altitude flying, as well as the great stress and danger of their work, are in need of occasional complete rest and relaxation." (Fold 3)

Towards the end of 1942, a number of country houses were requisitioned as rest homes for USAAF airmen. They were staffed and run by American Red Cross personnel who acted as hostesses, supervising recreation and dining facilities, supported by civilian staff from the local area to run the house and manage the grounds. They came under the jurisdiction of the 70th Replacement Depot HQ at Yarnfield.

In November 1942, the first of the 16 rest homes was opened. Stanbridge Earls (Station 505) was a large, historic country house and estate located a mile and a half north of Romsey in Hampshire. It was established to accommodate 30 officers from the 1st Air Division until the end of the war.

Other rest homes were: Walhampton House and Aylesfield House (both in Hampshire), Coombe House (Dorset), Furze Down (North Walsham), Buckland Hotel and Spetchley Park (Worcestershire), Keythorpe Hall (Leicestershire), Eynsham Hall and Moulesford Manor (Oxfordshire), Ebrington Manor (Cotsworlds), Pangbourne House (London), Roke Manor (Kent) and the last to be opened was Phyllis Court in Henley-on-Thames (see appendix for further details).

The temporary residents had a free choice of timetable and activities:

> "No attempt has been made to have the guest follow a fixed schedule of any kind. Every effort has been made to have all kinds of recreation available for them to use when and as they see fit." (Fold 3)

The houses had a number of facilities for the leisure of their occupants, usually including a music room with piano, radio and victrola; a library well stocked with books, magazines and newspapers; and a games room with table tennis, snooker and darts. The grounds of the house also had facilities available such as: tennis, badminton, cycling, softball, skeet (clay pigeon shooting), archery, swimming and boating. Sometimes it was possible to play golf or go horse-riding. Transport was usually available for residents to travel to nearby towns.

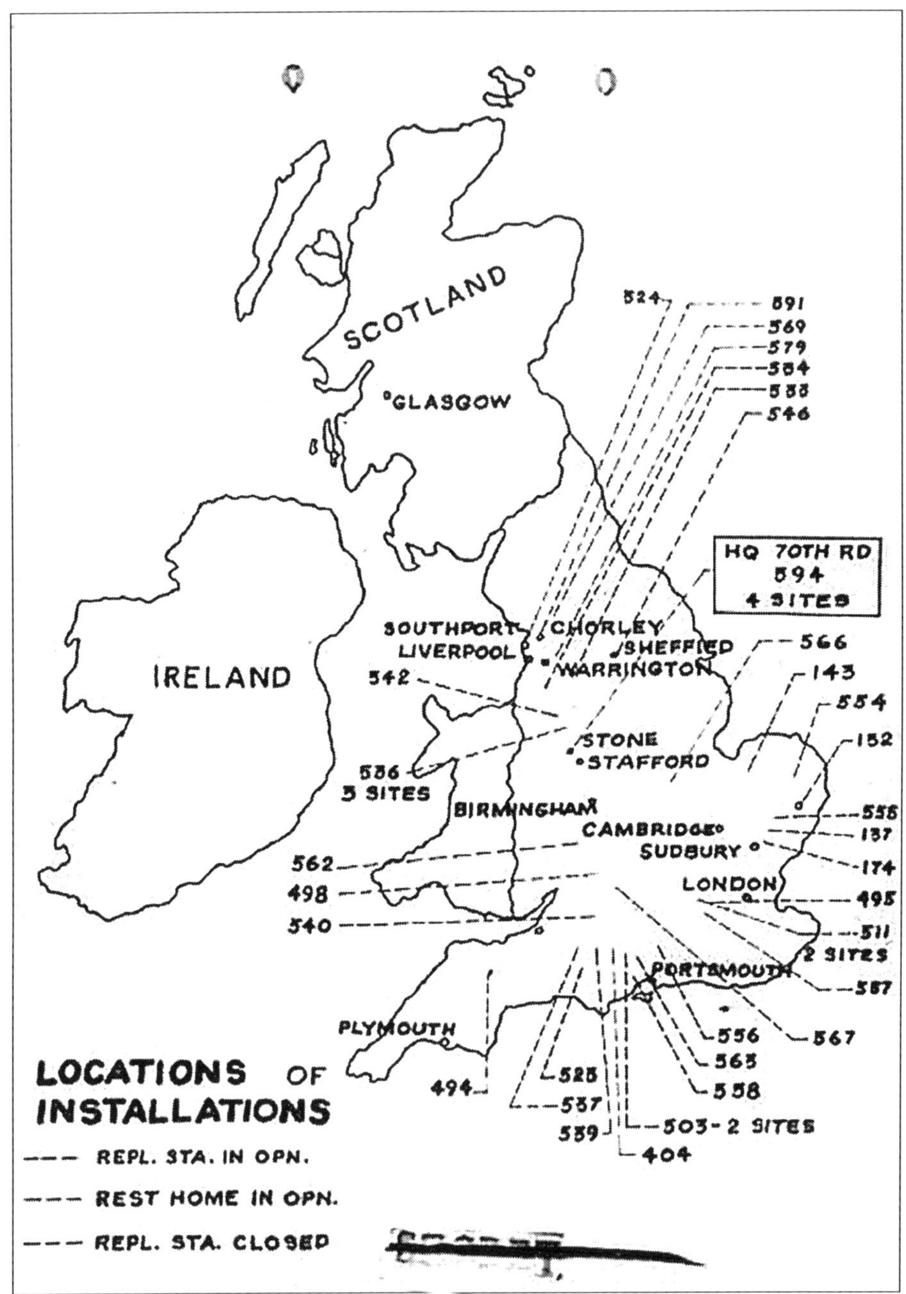

Locations of rest homes and other AAF installations. (Fold 3)

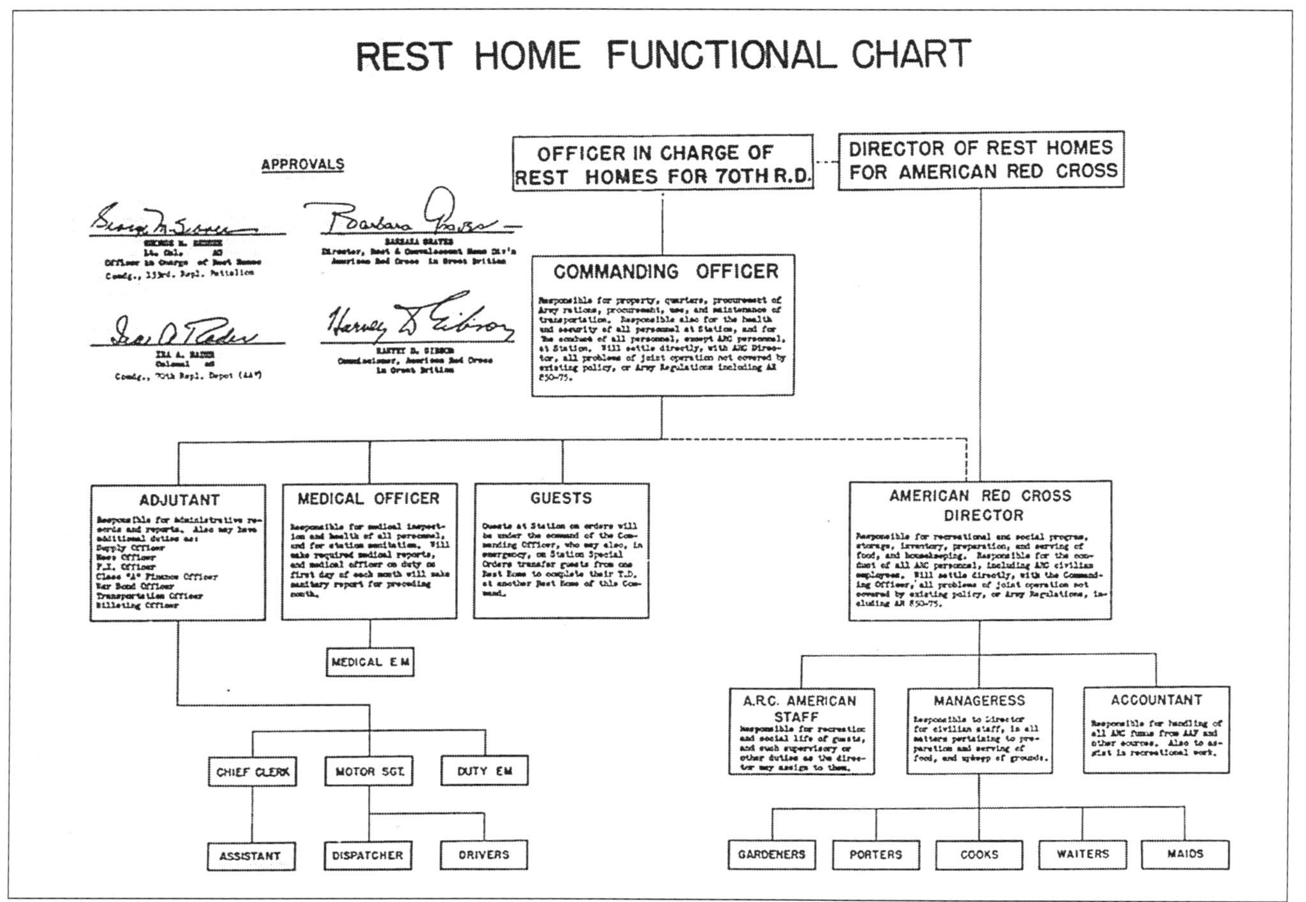
REST HOME FUNCTIONAL CHART
APPROVALS
OFFICER IN CHARGE OF REST HOMES FOR 70TH R.D.
DIRECTOR OF REST HOMES FOR AMERICAN RED CROSS
COMMANDING OFFICER
ADJUTANT
MEDICAL OFFICER
GUESTS
AMERICAN RED CROSS DIRECTOR
MEDICAL E M
CHIEF CLERK
MOTOR SGT.
DUTY EM
ASSISTANT
DISPATCHER
DRIVERS
A.R.C. AMERICAN STAFF
MANAGERESS
ACCOUNTANT
GARDENERS
PORTERS
COOKS
WAITERS
MAIDS

(Fold 3)

HEADQUARTERS
UNITED STATES STRATEGIC AIR FORCES IN EUROPE
Office of the Commanding General

APO 633, U.S. Army
23 August 1944

SUBJECT: Mission of Air Force Rest Homes.

TO: See Distribution.

1. Numerous officers and men are arriving at Air Force Rest Homes without proper knowledge of the purpose and operation of these Homes. Indoctrination of combat crews by the unit Flight Surgeons with respect to the organic set up and purpose of rest homes will help them more fully to appreciate the homes from the start.

2. Air Force Rest Homes are provided for members of combat crews only. These homes are operated under the Headquarters of the Eight Air Force Replacement Depot, and each has a commanding officer and staff. Members of combat crews are sent to these homes on temporary duty by their unit commanding officers on the recommendation of the unit Flight Surgeons.

3. Although A Rest Home is a military organization, the atmosphere is one of relaxation, recreation, and refinement, where there are no military duties, and the only restrictions placed on a guest are those which are necessary in consideration for the group as a whole.

4. The American Red Cross is an integral part of the program, supplying specially trained hostesses and employing and directing the civilian staff necessary to operate the homes. Without the splendid cooperation of the American Red Cross the program could not exist. The American Red Cross personnel extend their entire effort to make the guests' stay pleasant.

5. The mission of the Air Force Rest Home program is to return members of the combat crews to their units refreshed and physically and mentally rested.

6. To avoid wasting space officers responsible for bookings will make every effort to insure that rest home beds are utilized to the fullest extent according to their respective allotments.

7. In order that combat crewmen may secure the maximum benefit from their stay at a rest home unit commanders will require them to arrive promptly according to their orders and, providing the military situation permits, will authorise a minimum stay of seven days exclusive of travel time.

By command of Lieutenant General SPAATZ:

/s/ E. A. Mohley
/t/ E. A. MOHLEY
Lt. Col., AGD,
Asst. Adj. Gen.

DISTRIBUTION: D(Less AFSC and ASC Stations)

Incl #11

~~SECRET~~

Mission of rest homes. (Fold 3)

XXIII - OFFICER IN CHARGE OF REST HOME PROGRAM

The Officer in Charge of the Rest Home program is responsible for the following problems:

1. To maintain proper and uniform standards of Rest Home operation.

2. To locate and activate new Rest Homes and to reach, and remain at, authorised guest capacity.

3. To interpret present approved policies to Rest Home operating personnel.

4. To suggest new policies to higher authority for approval, as need for new or changed policies is indicated.

5. To maintain close contact with the American Red Cross.

6. To maintain liaison with Training and Organization Division, ASC, USSTAF.

7. To maintain liaison with Air Ministry to extent authorized.

8. To maintain liaison with operational group and division booking agencies.

9. To perform appropriate duties of military administration for organisation to which assigned.

Responsibilities of Officer in charge of rest homes. (Fold 3)

Colonel Radar, Lt. Col. Sebree and rest home officers. (Yarnfield Yank)

(Yarnfield Yank)

(Yarnfield Yank)

(Yarnfield Yank)

(Yarnfield Yank)

(Yarnfield Yank)

Chapter 8

'Cold and Aloof' English People?

THE PERMANENT staff and casuals at the 70th RD had both the time and opportunity to spend in the area around the replacement depot in Yarnfield. A number of personnel enjoyed watching the greyhound racing, which was probably at Monmore Green, Wolverhampton. There were also organised tours for the men and women to visit the various buildings such as the waterworks in Stone, which was toured by a group of officers in June 1944.

Dog Races. (Yarnfield Yank)

On Whit Sunday 1943, an American forces band played the music for a Red Cross Garden Fête at Aston Hall, on the outskirts of Stone. The opening ceremony was conducted by Viscountess Levenhulme, who was supported by Sir Ernest and Lady Johnson, Sir Ralph and Lady Wedgewood, Mrs Lionel Meakin and Miss Parker Jarvis, OBE. The event concluded with a dance at the village hall in the evening. A month later, in July 1943, a group of WACs from Jefferson Hall were invited to a tea party at Aston Hall by Mrs H.C. Wenger.

USAAF crew with Barclays Bank Manager, Mr Cyril Harrison. (David Welch)

Local residents after playing tennis with a GI from Yarnfield, Otto Schreister. (K. Lloyd)

George Edwards age 13–14 with a GI named Joe at Swynnerton. (Anthony Edwards)

Red Cross Garden Fete

At the Red Cross garden fete to be held at Aston Hall, near Stone, on Whit Monday, Viscountess Leverhulme, who will perform the opening ceremony, will be supported by Sir Ernest and Lady Johnson, Sir Ralph and Lady Wedgwood, Mrs. Lionel Meakin and Miss Parker-Jervis, O.B.E.

In addition to a variety of stalls, the attractions will include music by a band of the American Forces, a baby show, a bowling competition, pony rides for children, displays by Army Cadets and the Girls' Training Corps, sketches by school children, and dancing displays.

The event will conclude with a dance at the Aston Village Hall at night.

Evening Sentinel *7/6/1943.*

Angeline 'Frankie' Frank. (Wisconsin Vets Museum)

The 70th were also on hand to help the community when needed. In October 1943, the British authorities were struggling to complete refuse collections because of the increase in rubbish produced by the base at Jefferson Hall. In this case, personnel were able to help with the collections. A further refuse problem caused by servicemen in the area occurred because US servicemen were disposing of live ammunition in the refuse. This resulted in a number of small explosions at council tips. Members of the public were subsequently advised not to trespass on the disposal sites.

On the whole, the men and women of the 70th Replacement Depot enjoyed a good relationship with the local people. A number of men and women from Jefferson Hall were offered hospitality from the residents in the community. WAC, Angeline Frank recalls that an English priest came to the base to invite a servicewoman to visit one of the local families. When Angeline visited the Jordans at their house, she felt at home straight away. Her hostess gave her a vase with a country cottage scene on it that had been her mother's and insisted that Angeline send it to her mother so that she would know that her daughter was spending time with a family and not be so worried about her. Angeline felt like an adopted member of Jack and Mabel Jordan's family and was even invited to join them and their two daughters on a family holiday in Rhyl, which she took a furlough to do.

Another WAC, Beulah Johnson, also found 'a home away from home' with a local family from Hanley, the Triggs. Mrs Betty Trigg wrote to Beulah's mother in July 1944:

> "You will be pleased to hear that I have had the pleasure of entertaining your daughter, Beulah, for a short time. She is well and happy and is stationed at a very nice spot not far from a small country town. - - - Both my husband and I were very pleased to have Beulah stay with us, as we have 3 sons but all are away from home. I know how a mother feels when her children are far away from home, it is nice for me to have someone to mother." (Beulah's letters, Laura Ellis Lai)

In a later letter she wrote:

> "I shall miss all the girls when they return to the States. I have had some very happy hours with them. It has been quite a labour of love looking after them - - -. I tell all of them I hope they won't forget me when they return home but I shall have some very happy memories." (Beulah Johnson's letters, Laura Ellis Lai)

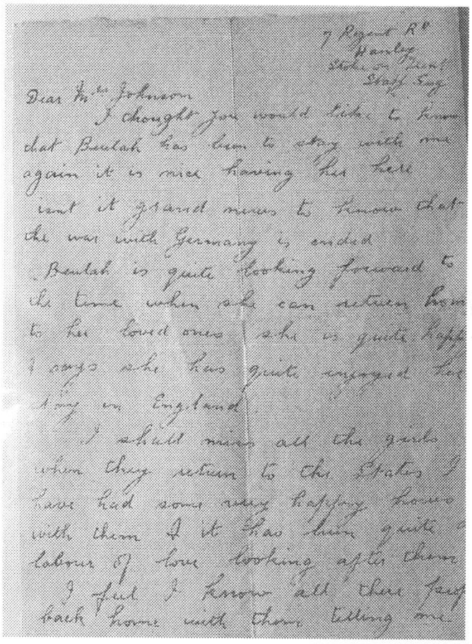

7 Regent Rd
Hanley
Stoke-on-Trent
Staffs Eng

Dear Mrs Johnson
I thought you would like to know that Beulah has been to stay with me again it is nice having her here isn't it grand news to know that the war with Germany is ended Beulah is quite looking forward to the time when she can return home to her loved ones she is quite happy & says she has quite enjoyed her stay in England
I shall miss all the girls when they return to the States I have had some very happy hours with them & it has been quite a labour of love looking after them
I feel I know all their folks back home with them telling me

Christmas was a chance for the men and women of the 70th to repay the hospitality that had been offered to them by the local people in Yarnfield and Stone. George Pearson remembers that the American servicemen were very kind to the children in the town, often giving them sweets and gum. For Christmas 1943, around 100 children who had been selected by various churches in the area were given a Christmas party on the base by the Americans. The previous year they did something similar as Richard Butler, one of the casuals, wrote in a V-mail in December 1942:

> "They're having a Xmas party here on the post for a bunch of kids around here." (*P-38 Odyssey* – Dick Butler)

The children were taken by bus to Jefferson Hall where they were received by Colonel Radar, who was accompanied by the Earl of Harrowby and the

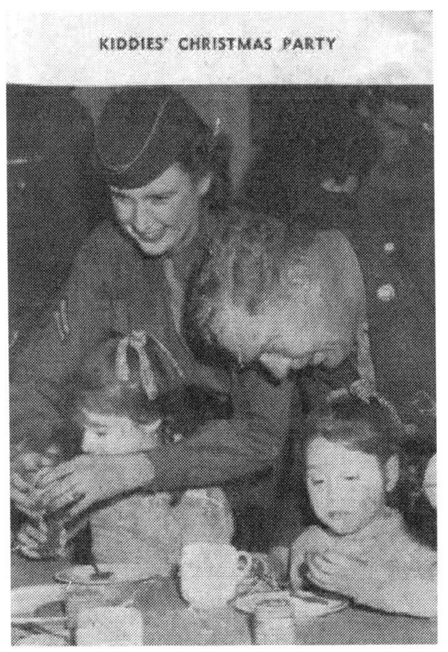
KIDDIES' CHRISTMAS PARTY

(Yarnfield Yank)

« SANTA CLAUS, I WANT... »

(Yarnfield Yank)

DONALD DUCK, MICKEY MOUSE AND PLUTO

(Yarnfield Yank)

(Yarnfield Yank)

John Howland. (Graham Bebbington)

Hon. Frances Ryder. After dinner, the children played games, watched cartoons and were presented with sweets, fruit juice, chocolate and two presents each from the large Christmas tree.

One of the casuals processed at the 70th, John Howland, from Carthage, Texas, arrived with his crew in Yarnfield a few days before Christmas 1943. He describes Christmas day at Jefferson Hall in his book, *Class of '43*.

> "The world was at war and it was Christmas Day 1943. The cooks at the Army

> Distribution Center, located near Stone, Staffordshire in Central England, had done their best to provide us with the military version of a Christmas dinner and all the trimmings. However, something was lacking that the finest cooks in the world couldn't serve. The atmosphere was subdued. Noise and clatter were missing as men went through the motions of eating the traditional turkey, stuffing and cranberry sauce. Perhaps they were lost in thoughts and memories of families, friends and loved ones several thousand miles away; or could they have been pondering the fate of the three crews lost out of our group during the flight across the North Atlantic Ocean, just one week earlier.
>
> With time on our hands following the sumptuous mid-day meal, and nothing better to do, my pilot, Jim Tyson and I walked four miles from the US Army Distribution Center into the town of Stone. The skies were dull grey and there was a damp chill in the air. The streets were empty and not a word was said between us as we wondered aimlessly in the general direction of a church we could see in the distance. Somehow the calm, peaceful tranquility of the setting in a country ravaged by war for more than four years seemed completely out of step with the frenzied hectic pace we had been following for more than one year." (*Class of '43* by John Howland)

As the two airmen walked along the road in Stone, a middle-aged woman approached them and invited them to Christmas tea with her family. The men gratefully accepted and walked towards the lady's parents' home where there was a full house. The lady's father was the director of John Joules Brewery. The two men were made to feel very welcome.

> "Conversation flowed freely. The tea and scones were delicious and we were treated with a warmth and friendship we hadn't seen since leaving home." (*Class of '43* by John Howland)

On leaving to return to base, the lady's two teenage children offered to take the men on a sightseeing tour of the area the following day if duties permitted. That evening, at the depot, two other casual airmen, Frank Palenik and Bob Laux had a similar tale to share about what had happened to them on Christmas Eve. While the two men were wandering through Stone, feeling lonely, a 12-year-old girl had approached them and invited them to visit her family, the Phillipses (Mr Phillips was the town constable).

The family insisted that the two airmen stay for a traditional Christmas Eve supper. At first the men were reluctant to stay, as they had been warned about the severe effect rationing was having on British households. However, the family were missing their son who was serving in North Africa with the RAF and it helped them to think they were giving hospitality to someone else's sons. They were especially pleased that Bob was able to fix their daughter's electric train set which had stopped working four years previously.

On Boxing Day, the clerks at Jefferson Hall were still typing Howland and Tyson's assignment orders so they were able to meet the two teenagers they had met the previous day. They were walked around all the potteries and given a history of each famous potter.

Two days after Christmas, the men received their orders assigning them to 535th Squadron of the 381st Bomb Group based at Ridgewell, Essex. They were replacements for some of the nine crews and 90 men lost to enemy action by the 381st during December. As they went to their new assignment, Howland wondered:

> "- - - where to find the 'cold and aloof' English people we had heard so much about. They certainly weren't part of this group" [of people we had met]. (*Class of '43* by John Howland)

Fifty years after the end of the war, Howland returned to Stone with a Texan flag and a formal proclamation from the city of Carthage declaring Carthage and Stone sister cities. Howland gave the flag as a reminder of the lasting friendship and appreciation of the people of Stone by the people of Carthage. The status of 'honorary Texans' was conferred on all the citizens of Stone. Howland stipulated that he wished the flag to be flown in Stone on festive occasions.

Chapter 9

In the Company of American Soldiers

INEVITABLY THERE were a number of romances between the GIs at Jefferson Hall and girls in the local area. There were several GI marriages. Surprisingly, one of them involved a WAAC from the base, Private Elizabeth Elliot of Kingston, North Carolina. She had been engaged to Sergeant Wallace R. Best of Raleigh, also in North Carolina before they came to England. They met up again when Elizabeth arrived in England as part of the first separate battalion of the WAAC to arrive in the UK. When Best heard that his fiancée was arriving in Stone, in July 1943, he requested a 48-hour pass from the commanding officer at his base 50 miles away, to go and greet her. Elizabeth became the first WAC bride in the ETO on 7 October 1943.

ETO's First WAC Bride To Wed Old Sweetheart

Pvt. Mary Elizabeth Elliott, of Kingston, N.C., will become the first WAC bride in this theater when she says "I do" to Sgt. Wallace R. Best, of Raleigh, N.C., next Thursday, Oct. 7, at an Eighth Air Force station where she has been on duty since her arrival with the first WAC expeditionary force.

The couple became engaged in the United States and met here at a replacement depot the day Pvt. Elliott arrived. Sgt. Best had a hunch his fiancee might be with the first WAC group and was on hand to greet her.

The ceremony will be performed by the Rev. G. M. Napier. Pfc Dorothy Whinery, of Anoka, Minn., will be maid of honour; Maj. William H. Buck will be best man, and Maj. Jacob W. Frederick, of Wakarusa, Ind., will give away the bride. Pfc Jane Elise Hastings, of Washington, and Pfc Olive Spencer, of Aliquippa, Pa., will provide wedding music.

Stars and Stripes *30/9/1943.*

Local man, George Pearson remembers that Sergeant Hansen, who later became Deputy Sheriff of Portland, Oregon, married a girl he met at a dance in the Potteries. When he met the girl, he told George that he knew he would marry her – and he did. After the war, the couple returned to the UK to visit family every couple of years. Sisters, Phyllis and Nancy Greatrex also married GIs from Yarnfield, one surnamed Scott and one surnamed Kapec. Both girls were married at Swynnerton Catholic Church. After the War, one sister moved to Boston and the other Pennsylvania.

One of the Greatrex sisters, with her beau and wedding photo.

At the end of the war, on 11 October 1945, a party was held by the Special Service of Duncan Hall for over 50 GI brides and their husbands. The venue was The Grand Hotel in Hanley. A special cake was baked in their honour and cut by Colonel Radar, who was presenting along with Major D.T. Robinson (Adjutant General) and Miss Margaret Carrol (Director of the American Red Cross Club in Hanley). The brides came mainly from North Staffordshire: Cobridge, Stafford, Tunstall, Abbey Hulton, Trent Vale, Eccleshall, Newcastle-under-Lyme, Sneyd Green, Fenton, Shelton, Norton, Weston Coyney, Etruria, Basford, Malton and Trentham.

Each couple received a souvenir programme of the event which had room to record their own and the other brides' English and American addresses so that they could keep in touch. There was talk of forming a 'Mayflower Club' for the girls to support each other when living in the States. Eight of the girls were to make their home in New York, three in California and one lady from Stone was moving to Massachusetts.

A number of the US personnel from Yarnfield and the surrounding areas, built relationships with local girls. Private Dwight Ellwood Young was based at Meaford Hall with the 35th Evacuation Hospital when he met local girl, Winnifred Parfitt, who was working as a wages clerk at ROF Swynnerton. He had enlisted

Americans' Wives

HANLEY PARTY

Upwards of 50 young married couples—English wives and their American husbands—were last night entertained to a dinner-dance at the Grand Hotel, Hanley, by the Special Service Division of the U.S.A. Army Air Force stationed at Duncan Hall, Stone.

Nearly all of the brides were North Staffordshire girls, and the function afforded a happy opportunity of their getting-together and, in some cases even, of meeting future "near neighbours" in the States.

The outcome may be the formation of a Mayflower Club for local brides awaiting passage across the Atlantic to their new homes. Some of the husbands are shortly going back home or to the continent.

Each couple received a souvenir programme of the occasion which, bearing the warm title of "Uncle Sam's New Chillun—and where they will live," recorded their names and their English and American addresses in directory fashion.

The New Homes

No fewer than eight local girls, according to the directory, will make their homes in New York. For three others it will be a case of "California, here I come." One Stone girl, at least, will have to get used to spelling Massachusetts.

Other brides come from Hanley, Cobridge, Stafford, Tunstall, Abbey Hulton, Trent Vale, Eccleshall, Newcastle, Sneyd Green, Fenton, Shelton, Norton, Weston Coyney, Etruria, Basford, Milton and Trentham.

A special cake was made in their honour and cut by the Commanding Officer, Colonel I. A. Rader, who was present with Major D. T. Robinson (Adjutant-General) and Miss Margaret Carroll (Director of the American Red Cross Club in Hanley).

In short speeches, Colonel Rader contrasted every-day life in America and Britain; and Miss Carroll, suggesting the formation of a bride's or Mayflower Club, extended a cordial invitation to local wives of American servicemen to a meeting at the Red Cross Club on Monday, for the purpose of inaugurating such a club.

Arrangements for the event

Staffordshire Sentinel *12/10/1945.*

Private Dwight Ellwood Young with a bottle of the local Joules Beer. (Kathleen Robinson)

in the US Army in 1941, at which point he was assigned to serve with the 29th Medical Training Battalion. Unfortunately, when Private Young left Meaford Hall in 1944, he did not realise that he had left Winnifred pregnant. Baby Kathleen was born in March 1945 and sadly was destined never to meet her father.

Dwight had previously given his girlfriend a photo of him and an ID bracelet with his name and service number on, so, in 1994, after her mother's death, Kathleen was able to use these as a starting point to trace her family in the United States. She obtained her father's medical records and learned that although he had survived the Second World War, sadly, he had died after an accident in 1951 when serving in the Korean War. His army record also gave details of his family members and after some more years of research, she posted the family details on Ancestry and in 2016 she was contacted by one of her American cousins.

Kathleen was able to contact a number of members of the family who had previously not known of her existence but were delighted to find out about her and wanted to meet her and welcome her into the family. Later that year, she travelled to America, meeting family in Wichita, California and her father's birthplace, Aline, Oklahoma. She was also able to visit his grave. Since then, some of her cousins have visited her in the UK.

Corporal John Brooks from Columbus, Ohio, a member of the 1257th MP Battalion, met his future wife, Josephine Bott, in the Crown Hotel, in Stone, where she was a wine steward. The couple were married in January 1946. John was discharged from the US Army in May but remained in England at the Temperance Hotel in Stone, until August.

Sadly, when he returned to America, he returned alone, as his wife's family put pressure on her to stay in the UK. Later, Josephine moved to London, but her son, Michael, stayed in Stone with the extended family. John wrote frequently to Josephine, at her mother's address, but she didn't receive the letters as her mother threw them in the fire instead of forwarding them to her.

John always kept a photo of his wife with him and regretted that they had not stayed together. His family in the US knew all about the wife and child

John Brooks and Josephine Bott. (Nick Brooks)

he had left behind and when John died in 1975, his sister travelled to Stone to tell the family the sad news. She met members of the family who still lived in Mill Street and tracked down Josephine, living in London, to inform her. Josephine always found the meeting too painful to discuss.

Unfortunately, the two families didn't keep in touch and eventually lost contact. In 2018, John and Josephine's grandson, Nick, managed to track down the American side of the family through American year books of schools in the area and by using Ancestry.com and Facebook. He was able to visit his 26 newly-found relations in Ohio and the following year, his grandfather's daughter (his father's stepsister) and her children came to visit him in the UK.

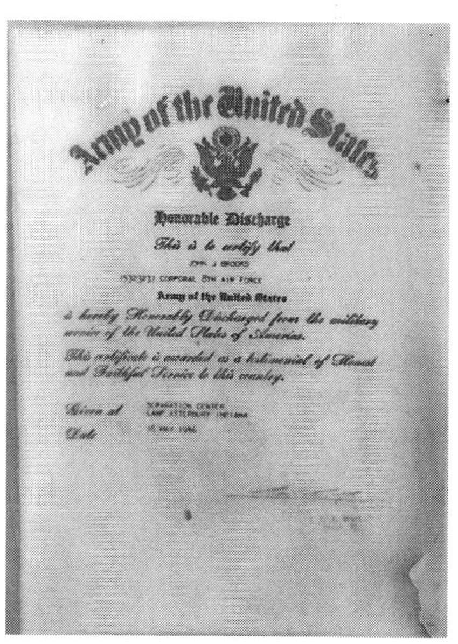

Army of the United States

Honorable Discharge

This is to certify that

Army of the United States

is hereby Honorably Discharged from the military service of the United States of America.

This certificate is awarded as a testimonial of Honest and Faithful Service to this country.

Given at

Date

John Brook's discharge papers. (Nick Brooks)

Another romance between a GI and a local girl (who was an engraver in Stone) also ended sadly. The girl's parents had forbidden her to date GIs, but nevertheless, she dated and fell in love with 19-year-old, Ed. Eventually, he visited her house and met her parents, but her father was still unhappy about the relationship. She asked her father if they could get engaged but he ignored her and refused to answer. The couple decided to go ahead and bought a ring in Hanley, but when the girl's father noticed it on her finger, he threw it in the fire. A loud argument ensued, but when everyone had calmed down, the ring was retrieved from the fire and the father reluctantly agreed to the engagement.

The next problem for the couple to overcome, was the question of religion, as she was a Catholic and Ed was Episcopalian. It was necessary for the couple to have interviews with the priest, the base padre and the commanding officer. It was also mandatory to fill in numerous forms. Ed's parents in the USA even had to complete an affidavit to say that they would take responsibility for the girl while she lived in the US.

Plans for the wedding were made and a cake with soya flour in the place of marzipan was baked. While the preparations were going ahead, a group of men from the base, including Ed, were assigned to Camp Griffiss, Bushy Park, in Surrey. A couple of weeks later, Ed managed to get back to Staffordshire on a pass. He was able to see his fiancée briefly and warn her that he wouldn't be able to visit for a while although he didn't explain why. A few days later, the Normandy landings took place and the girl realised why Ed had been so secretive.

Only one letter arrived from Ed in the next few months, so the girl was unable to find out what had happened to him. At Christmas time, they ate the wedding cake which was becoming discoloured due to the soya flour. The next time the girl heard from Ed, she found out that he had been discharged from the army and was back in the US. He had made a girl pregnant so he had married her. Two years later, another letter arrived, explaining that he had divorced his first wife so he would be free to marry her now. By this time, she had got married herself so she declined the offer.

In October 1943, the *Stone Advertiser* and the *Stafford Advertiser* reported on the tragic ending of the relationship between 24-year-old 2nd Lieutenant Norman H. Goldberg and 19-year-old Irene Hawkins from Cold Meece.

The couple, who were drinking at the Crown Hotel with another couple, 23-year-old 2nd Lieutenant James W. LaVoie and Joyce Norman, left the pub at 9.00pm intending to go to St Joseph's Hall to attend a dance run by the American Red Cross. Unfortunately, they lost their way in the blackout and by mistake, they walked through the gasworks yard. In the dark, Miss Norman fell in the canal, but was able to scramble to safety.

The group turned back and made their way back through the gasworks in the dark, when Lieutenant Goldberg and Miss Hawkins walked into a disused gas holder sump. Miss Norman ran for help while Lieutenant LaVoie made a make-shift rope out of his jacket for them to hang on to. The rescue was made difficult because the surface of the water was so far below ground level. The sump was 30 ft deep and contained 12 to 15 ft of water. Another US soldier jumped into the water to try and save the couple but was unsuccessful.

BLACK-OUT TRAGEDY AT STONE

American Officer Drowned

An American Air Force officer, Second-Lieut. Norman H. Goldberg (24) was drowned, and his companion, Irene Wilhelmina Hawkins (19) Cold Meece, Stone, narrowly escaped drowning when they fell into a disused gasometer sump in the gasworks yard at Stone on Saturday night. The sump is about 36 feet in diameter and 30 feet deep, and contained 12 to 15 feet of water.

Lieut. Goldberg and Miss Hawkins were accompanied by another American officer, Second-Lieut. James W. La Voie (23) and Miss Joyce Norman, Manor Rise, Walton, and about 9 p.m. they were making their way to a dance at St. Joseph's Hall. Mistaking their way in the black-out, they went through the gasworks yard and reached the canal towing path. In the darkness, Miss Norman stumbled into the canal but managed to scramble out. The party were retracing their steps through the gasworks yard when the tragedy occurred, both Lieut. Goldberg and Miss Hawkins walking into the sump.

Rescue attempts were rendered extremely difficult owing to the distance separating the surface of the water from the ground level. Miss Hawkins, who is a swimmer, managed to keep afloat, but she was unconscious when rescued. She has since made a good recovery. When Lieut. Goldberg was taken from the water he was dead.

Staffordshire Sentinel *25/10/1943.*

Eventually, Miss Hawkins was pulled out unconscious but she subsequently made a full recovery. Meanwhile a War Reserve Police Constable found a ladder and was able to recover the body of Lieutenant Goldberg by tying a rope around his waist. Dr C. Arthur of Stone attempted to resuscitate the man but was unsuccessful. An enquiry into the fatality was held at Jefferson Hall with a verdict of 'Accidental Death' recorded.

Not all of the liaisons between the airmen of the 70th and the local girls were considered 'romantic' in nature. There are at least two reports from the *Staffordshire Sentinel* in 1944 informing their readership of court cases of underage girls frequenting venues alongside American soldiers.

The first was in January 1944, when Norma Cox, aged 17, was summoned to Stone Police Court for purchasing 'intoxicating liquor' at the White Lion in High Street, Stone. The report also includes the comment:

> "Also present in the room, were American soldiers and other girls." (*Staffordshire Sentinel* 5/1/1944)

GIRL'S CAFE VISITS

STATEMENT TO MAGISTRATE

When the Potteries Stipendiary Magistrate (Mr. R. Macgregor Clarkson) at a Juvenile Court, at Fenton yesterday, committed a 16-years-old Meir girl to an approved school for failure to comply with a three years supervision order made against her on May 17th last, he requested that certain allegations made in respect of a roadside cafe between the Potteries and Stone should be investigated by the appropriate authorities.

Superintendent H. Edge, of Longton, stated that the girl had been away from home for 12 days since the supervision order was made against her on May 17th last. She had caused her parents considerable trouble, and they were unable to exercise any proper control over her. The girl had been in the company of American soldiers, and had several times been reported to the police as missing from home.

Girl's Statement

Replying to questions by Mr. Clarkson, the girl stated that, for most of the time while she was away from home, she spent the nights at a roadside cafe between the Potteries and Stone, where girls went with American soldiers. She stated that she and other girls, who usually numbered about eight, went to the cafe about 10.30 at night, and stayed in a little side room until about 3.30 in the morning. The girls often slept in this room, and at about 3.30 a.m. they left the premises and had a walk round.

Mr. Clarkson: Does the cafe owner provide this room for sleeping purposes?

The girl: No, he does not know we sleep there. We collect and pay for our own food.

The Problem

Staffordshire Sentinel *15/6/1944.*

Apparently, the girl lied three times to the publican, telling him she was 18. In her defence, she explained that she was accompanying her sister who was meeting her boyfriend and she had said she was 18 as she thought she wouldn't be allowed in otherwise. She was put on probation for three years and ordered to pay costs. The second report from the *Staffordshire Sentinel* was from June 1944 and was a little more serious. A 16-year-old from Meir was in the juvenile court for the Potteries because she had spent a number of nights at a roadside café between the Potteries and Stone:

> "- - - in the company of American soldiers." (*Staffordshire Sentinel* 15/6/1944)

The girl had been reported to the police as 'missing' several times. Apparently, she and a group of other girls regularly visited the café around 10.30pm and stayed there in a side room until about 3.30am. When the magistrate, Mr Clarkson, pointed out that the girl in court was just 16, Superintendent Edge replied that he had taken this and other cases up with the American military authorities, but their answer was always that they could not keep the girls away from the American troops. The girl was committed to an approved school as her parents were:

> "unable to exercise any proper control over her." (*Staffordshire Sentinel* 15/6/1944)

It was also decided that the details should be passed on to the Stone Police Force to investigate the activities at the café more rigorously.

Chapter 10

Celebrations and Farewells

WHEN VE Day was declared on 8 May 1945, both the people of Stone and its temporary American residents, made plans to celebrate. In the town, street parties were held with bunting strung between properties and flags hung from bedroom windows.

Evening Sentinel — CITY FINAL

END OF EUROPEAN WAR

Surrender Signed at Rheims This Morning

HISTORIC EVENT EISENHOWER'S HEADQUARTERS

Churchill's Broadcast Very Soon

It is officially announced that Germany has surrendered unconditionally.

The capitulation document was signed at 2.41 a.m. to-day (French time) in a little school house at Rheims, which is General Eisenhower's Headquarters.

The German Surrender In Norway

How Surrender Was Announced by Germans

Body Of Gobbels Found

MOSCOW REPORT

CASUALTIES ON WAR FRONTS

The Polish Issue

DEEP CONCERN IN LONDON

LAST ACT OF TERROR FOILED

DACHAU ORDER BY HIMMLER

Evening Sentinel *7/5/1945.*

VE Day prayers at Jefferson Hall. (Yarnfield Yank)

Milton Cook, of the 1257th MP Battalion, was scheduled to be off-duty on this day and so had made plans to celebrate. Unfortunately, his platoon was designated a stand-by unit in case of disorder. Cook thought the platoon was unlikely to be required as it was doubtful whether the celebrating servicemen would be able to procure enough alcohol to cause trouble because of the demand on the local pubs from local people.

Fortunately, when Cook had been assigned to collect an AWOL serviceman from Paris, he had brought back a bottle of champagne to keep for such an occasion. He informed his platoon that they should collect their canteen cups and a toast was made to victory with the

Colonel Radar joining men in a game as part of VE day celebrations on base. (Yarnfield Yank)

warm bottle of cheap champagne which was divided between the aluminum cups. When the champagne was finished, the men shared the cheap cognac Cook had also brought back with him.

The men decided to march to the mess hall to find something to eat, singing the popular British song of the time, *I've got sixpence*, followed by *I've been working on the railroad*. When an MP from another platoon asked where the alcohol had come from, he was told that it was a military secret. The mess hall officers were unwilling to give the rowdy group of men access to the mess hall and threatened to call the MPs, to which the men replied, "We are the MPs!". Reluctantly they gave them something to eat. Cook reflects that they probably weren't in the best of shape to put down a riot, but they probably would have enjoyed doing it. He wrote:

> "The only group of imbibing GIs which we were almost called on to deal with, was us." (*That's the Way the Ball Bounces* – Milton Cook)

Celebrations in the area surrounding the base were mostly peaceful. The only unrest linked to the American soldiers was an outbreak of fighting at the Duke of York pub in Mill Meece between US troops and Canadians training at nearby HMS Fledgling. Apparently, the fighting started after a debate as to which country had contributed most to win the war.

Meaty Objection

I am at the 70th Reinforcement Depot and have been waiting to be ZId for the last month. Whenever we leave here we all have to pay our mess bills in cash at the rate of four shillings per day, regardless of the time spent on pass.

This seems like a nice racket, with approximately 2.000 officers a month passing through here, and probably 50 per cent of their time spent on pass.

Isn't one allowed to declare his meals and pay for just what he eats?—1/*Lt. Glenn J. Smart. 52nd Ftr. Control Sq.*

Letter of complaint in Stars and Stripes *12/7/1945.*

VE Day was also celebrated at Washington Hall in Lancashire where it was said that a number of celebratory bonfires in the area were burning, amongst other items, the administration office furniture.

After VE Day, the 70th continued to process personnel at maximum capacity. The depots were busier than ever because of the number of air bases closing down and troops that were surplus to requirement in the European Theatre of Operations. During this time, the priority for the 70th was to repatriate airmen back to the US.

HEADQUARTERS
70TH REPLACEMENT DEPOT (AAF)
APO 652

JUL 13 1945
Date

AIR TRAVEL CLEARANCE CERTIFICATE

Philip A. Walter — 0704994 — Capt.
NAME — ASN — GRADE

I certify that above-named personnel has been processed and cleared as of 1700 hours, JUL 13 1945 19__ for air shipment to the United States (or transfer to another Theater of Operations) in compliance with Letter AG 370.5 (Short Title: PHI) 16 August 1944, as amended, and current Theater directives.

All required records and allied papers have been duly processed and are in order, and are in the possession of the above-named personnel to whom they pertain.

CERTIFIED:
(Shipping Agency Clearance Officer)

Norman [illegible]
Name

Capt AC
Rank

Off [illegible] Sec
Office

CASUAL POOL 70th R.D. (AAF) STA 594
Organization

Note: This clearance certificate is to be turned in to ATC Priorities and Traffic ticket office at the time ticket for air transportation is picked up. Ticket will not be issued for personnel without this certificate.

This certificate may also be used for clearance of AAF tactical crews flying tactical aircraft. The footnote will then state that the certificate will be turned into ATC Operations or SAS Embarkation Officer at the ATC receiving station upon arrival of crew from Theater staging area.

The handling will indicate, instead of name of individual, the appropriate crew number and plane number.

70th RD TMO 352

Air Travel Clearance for airman to be repatriated. (Fold 3)

Before VE Day, each morning, the MP Company had been forming in ranks for roll call, however, after VE Day, there were always large numbers missing: some on duty; some on furlough; some had been released to Nelson Hall for continuous gate duty; and some were detached to other stations. The morning roll call dwindled and eventually ended altogether. By this time, street lights in the UK had been lit again and blackout curtains had become redundant. On 23 May WAC Beulah Johnson wrote home to her parents:

> "Now that the firing has ceased in Europe we are beginning to wonder what next. The only thing I am sure of is that we will not be coming home for some time to come."

On VJ night, further celebrations took place across Staffordshire. In Hanley, a bonfire was lit in the middle of the square and loud celebrations continued into the early hours to the accompaniment of drums and cornets. One GI and his girlfriend climbed onto the roof of a bus parked in Market Street and danced to the music. Another GI climbed on a lamp standard to hoist both the Union Jack and the Stars and Stripes flags, then he hung his cap on top of the flags. Servicemen of other nations, such as Britain, Holland and the Caribbean, followed suit. A police sergeant was lifted shoulder high by a different GI and carried around the square. His helmet was also removed and placed on a lamp standard.

WAC, Angeline Frank, would have preferred to celebrate VJ Day with her adopted British family, but this was not to be as most of the servicemen and women from Jefferson Hall were confined to barracks. Whilst relaxing in the WAC quarters, Angeline heard a scream. Upon investigation, she saw a naked figure running down the hall. When the person turned around, she saw that it was not one of the WACs, as she had originally thought. The man

*VJ Day rejoicing at Jefferson Hall. (*Yarnfield Yank*)*

fled, chased by Angeline, and ended up in the arms of one of the MPs who carried him all the way to the guardhouse while he continually repeated, "Put me down, I'm an officer!" The next day, the WAC Commanding Officer, Lieutenant Kimmel, spoke to the WAC Battalion to inform them that the authorities had not discovered who the man was. She surmised that he may have been a prisoner of war from a nearby camp. That evening, the Charge of Quarters told the girls that it was actually one of the officers from Jefferson Hall. He was subsequently moved to another post, but brought back for the court martial at which occasion, Angeline was the main witness.

*Colonel John E. Clyde. (*Yarnfield Yank*)*

After VJ Day, the numbers of servicemen being processed through the depot began to fall. Even though the war was over, the MPs still had duties to carry out. Milton Cook was sent to London twice to collect AWOL personnel. He reflected:

> "Those two GIs who I had escorted back from London had, by going AWOL, most certainly extended their stay in England, or maybe in Europe." (*That's the Way the Ball Bounces* – Milton Cook)

Upon Cook's return from his last trip to London, he found that the depot had been reorganised. Colonel Radar was no longer the CO at Jefferson Hall, but was now Commanding Officer of Headquarters and Headquarters Company, 70th Reinforcement Depot (AAF). The depot of Jefferson Hall was now under the command of Colonel John E. Clyde. The new unit designation was: Headquarters AAF/ET Reinforcement Depot (PROV) (MAN). Orders were signed by the newly appointed Acting Assistant Adv. Gen, 1st Lieutenant Dorothy A. Kimmal.

COLONEL CLYDE'S STAFF

(Yarnfield Yank)

The longer serving staff at the 70th began returning to America as soon as they had enough points (gained from being overseas in the US Army) and those that had been stationed there for the shorter time, ran the depot. By mid-October, the last of the repatriating GIs had been sent to the Port of Embarkation for the sea journey back to the US. Because of the dwindling Service of Supply system, those that remained to the end, experienced some rationing shortages. Towards the end, the men were kept on short rations which consisted of left over K-rations supplemented with what could be acquired locally.

1st Lieutenant Dorothy A. Kimmal. (Yarnfield Yank)

On 8 October 1945, a farewell party was held at Washington Hall in Chorley for 350 USAAF staff, wives and friends. Lieutenant Colonel B.M. Prince, the then Commanding Officer, presented a plaque and flag to the people of the town who had welcomed the Americans who were so far from home. The flag was first marched through the town as part of a parade. Both items can still be seen in St Laurence's Church. The bronze plaque with the flag reads:

> "Presented by the US forces stationed at Washington Hall August 5th 1942 to October 10th 1945, in grateful appreciation of the hospitality extended by the citizens of Chorley and vicinity."

In 2021 Nancy Pelosi (US Speaker in the House of Representatives) visited the church and dedicated a new flag in remembrance of the wartime activities of the base.

heard by a Chorley man to say: "I hope we get back to Chorley soon." He thanked them for the job they had done, for the way they had fitted into our English life and customs and for the forbearance they had shown with the people who could not quite see eye to eye with them at first.

..."Presented by the U.S. Forces stationed at Washington Hall, August 5th, 1942 to October 10th, 1945, in grateful appreciation of the hospitality extended by the citizens of Chorley and vicinity." This is the inscription on the bronze plaque presented by the C.O. (Lieut.-Col. Prince) to the Mayor, Ald. J. Green, shortly before U.S. Forces left Chorley district. Also on the group are left, Lieut. J. M. Gordy; right, Major A. P. Aubuchon.

Presentation of plaque to Mayor of Chorley. (Stuart Clewlow)

Flag paraded through Chorley. (Stuart Clewlow)

Flag above Standish pew in St Laurence's Church. (Stuart Clewlow)

Flag in St Laurence's Church. (Stuart Clewlow)

Presentation of flag by Nancy Pelosi. (Stuart Clewlow)

US flag left at Washington Hall. (Stuart Clewlow)

Eventually only 50-60 members of the 1257th remained at Jefferson Hall. The point control post on the A34 was vacated and foot patrols ceased. Patrol duties in Mill Meece ended when Nelson Hall shut down. The depot at Jefferson Hall began the process of closing. Howard Hall held a farewell party for the local people on 14 October 1945. Beatty Hall was closed on 20 October and in the last week of October, the order was issued for the men to pack up and move into Duncan Hall. Howard Hall was closed on 1 November.

*Retreat at Jefferson Hall. (*Yarnfield Yank*)*

The 1257th MP Battalion became known as the 156th Reinforcement Company in the 130th Reinforcement Battalion. In the second week of November, the MPs were informed that they would not be returning directly home from the UK as they had a new assignment, although they were not told where it would be. On 15 November, Duncan Hall was shut down.

The MPs were transported to London and from there to Dover. They sailed to France and were assigned to Camp San Francisco, Château-Thierry, near Paris, which was to be the new location for the 1257th MP Battalion. At this point, the battalion reverted back to being known as the 1257th MP Battalion.

From France, the 1257th moved to Germany where they lived for two months at Fürstenfeldbruck Air Base in 'tent city'. In December, the group were given orders to move to the Port of Embarkation, stopping at Château Rothschild for a few days. Cook spent Christmas 1945 in a tent at Camp Lucky Strike near to Le Havre. On Boxing Day, Cook and his fellow MPs boarded USS *Mount Vernon* for the voyage home. Other members of the 70th travelled home on the *Queen Mary*.

*Retreat at Jefferson Hall. (*Yarnfield Yank*)*

*Cook at Camp Lucky Strike. (*That's the Way the Ball Bounces – *Milton Cook)*

Cook on return voyage on USS Vernon. *(*That's the Way the Ball Bounces – *Milton Cook)*

Queen Mary. *(*Yarnfield Yank*)*

Queen Mary. *(Yarnfield Yank)*

Epilogue

Post-War

AT THE end of the war, the buildings of the 70th Replacement Depot took on a new life. Adams Hall, at Bamber Bridge became a college for accelerated teacher training for ex-service people. One original hut, the former guardroom, remains and is still used.

Remaining hut at Adams Hall.

Washington Hall, in Chorley, became a rehabilitation centre for returning servicemen from Japanese POW camps. In 1948, it also took on the role of teacher training, retraining teachers who had returned from the armed forces. From 1954-1958, it became part of the Cold War MOD emergency programme, training RAF personnel in fire-fighting. In 1964, the site was handed over to Lancashire Fire and Rescue Service. Very little remains of the original buildings although some of the trees on the site still bear the names of the GIs who carved them there during the war.

Meanwhile in Stone, at the end of 1945, Nelson Hall was used for a short time by the American forces. In 1949, the County of Stafford Training College, known as Madeley College, was founded there. It was originally an all-female college for teacher training and domestic subjects. In 1958, the first male students were admitted. Physical Education teacher training became a

Adams Hall in the 1960s/1970s.

Washington Hall in the 1970s prior to the site being redeveloped by Lancashire Fire and Rescue. (Stuart Clewlow)

speciality and Madeley College led the field in the country in this subject. Due to government policies and the diminishing birth rate, in 1982 Madeley College was forced to close, its role being taken on by North Staffordshire Polytechnic. Nelson Hall was demolished and now lies under a housing estate.

Nelson Hall when it was a teacher training college c1970s.

Aerial view of Madeley College c1970s.

The three halls at Yarnfield were selected by the General Post Office as a venue for a new central training school which opened on 3 September 1946. In 1969, the GPO became the Post Office Corporation and in October 1981, Post Office Telephones became known as British Telecom.

In the 1970s there was some demolition work on the site to make space for purpose-built construction. During the demolition of Beatty Hall, sections of brickwork containing paintings from its time as a replacement depot, were uncovered when a false ceiling was removed in the former mess hall. The authorities contacted the military historian for the 3rd US Air Force who was stationed in the UK at RAF Mildenhall. Mr J. Heinz examined the mural, which had been painted by Sergeant Lew Sahilka, and carefully preserved it and framed the wall art in timber so that it could be transported to the National Museum of the US Air Force in Dayton, Ohio after a small flag-raising ceremony. The sections are still kept there today.

Part of mural. (Shaun Farrelly)

Part of mural. (National Museum of the US Air Force)

Part of mural. (National Museum of the US Air Force)

Part of mural. (National Museum of the US Air Force)

*Part of mural. (*Evening Sentinel *30/1/1982)*

(Express and Star *17/2/1977)*

The base at Yarnfield remained a British Telecom training centre until the summer of 2010, when it became a commercial conference centre known as Yarnfield Park. The centre has 40 event spaces and 338 bedrooms, making it one of the UK's largest centres. It is used as a training venue, conference centre and religious retreat. Although most of the original 1939 buildings have been demolished to make way for the purpose-built conference centre, a couple of small original buildings remain. On the Howard Hall site the steam-boiler building can still be seen. On the Duncan Hall site the sewage-pumping building is also still in existence.

*Flag-raising ceremony at the British Telecom Technical Training College. L-R: Mr Earl Heggie (college principal), Mr Norman Fox and Mr Jay Heinz (USAF historian). (*Evening Sentinel *30/1/1982)*

Steam-boiler building, Howard Hall (M. Collins) (Original building can be seen in Milton Cook's photo in chapter 5).

Acknowledgements

Individuals:

Graham Bebbington, David Beeby, Nick Brookes, Bill Bush, Veda Cook, Stuart Clewlow, Laura Ellis Lai, Shaun Farrelly, Jeff and Christine Goodwin, Gary Lea, Kathleen Robinson.

Publications:

Class of '43 by John Howland
Greenhorns and Happy Warriors by Euan Withersby
Memories of Stone by George Pearson
P-38 Odyssey by Dick Butler
Staffordshire Airfields by Alec Brew
Stars and Stripes
That's the Way the Ball Bounces by Milton Cook
The Battle of Bamber Bridge by Derek Rogerson
The GIs by Norman Longmate
Yarnfield Yank

Newspapers:

British Newspaper Archives – *Staffordshire Advertiser*, *Stone Advertiser*, *Staffordshire Newsletter*, *Staffordshire Sentinel*

Organisations and online sources:

Army Air Forces in World War 2 – Craven and Cate
Fold 3 – US Military Archives
Keele University (Helen Burton)
Leyland Historical Society (Peter Houghton)
National Museum of the US Air Force (Brett Stolle)
Second World War Experience Centre (Anne Wickes)
Staffordshire Past Track
Stone Library (Sheree Dearman)
Stuart Smith – World War 2 photos
Wisconsin Vets Museum (Jeff Javid)

Abbreviations

A.A.F. – Army Air Force
A.F.S.C. – Air Force Service Command
A.R.C. – American Red Cross
A.T.C. – Air Transport Control
A.W.O.L. – Absent Without Leave
C.O. – Commanding Officer
E.T.O. – European Theatre of Operations
E.T.O.U.S.A. – European Theatre of Operations, United States of America
H.Q. – Headquarters
M.P. – Military Police
M.T.O. – Mediterranean Theater of Operations
N.C.O. – Non-Commissioned Officer
Col. – Colonel
Cpl. – Corporal
Gen. – General
Lt. – Lieutenant
Maj. – Major
Pfc. – Private First Class
Pvt. – Private
Sgt. – Sergeant
Tec.4 – Technician 4th Grade
P.O.W. – Prisoner of War
P.X. – Post Exchange – (US equivalent of NAAFI)
R. and R. – Rest and Recuperation – spent at designated country houses
R.A.F. – Royal Air Force
R.C.A.F. – Royal Canadian Air Force
R.C.D. – Replacement Control Depot
R.D. – Replacement Depot (later known as Reinforcement Depot)
R.O.F. – Royal Ordnance Factory
S.O.S. – Services of Supply
U.S.A.A.F. – United States Army Air Force
U.S.A.F.B.I. – United States Army Forces in the British Isles

U.S.O. – United Service Organisation (US)
V.E. Day – Victory Europe Day
V.J. Day – Victory Japan Day
W.A.C./W.A.A.C. – Women's Army (Auxiliary) Corps (American) – known as Auxiliary until 1943
Comm. Z. – Communication Zone – area behind the combat zone, i.e. UK
Z.I. – Zone of the Interior (US)

Glossary

Assigned – having permanent duties at a base.

Unassigned – not officially attached to a unit or base.

Attached – personnel attached to a base.

Casual – personnel at a base for a short time while awaiting reassignment.

Detached – personnel on temporary assignment.

Donut Dugout – American Red Cross Club where coffee and doughnuts were served.

Limited Assignment – able to carry out limited duties (due to physical disability, etc).

Class A Uniform – formal dress uniform.

Mess Hall – canteen on a US military base.

Motor Pool – unit that repaired and maintained the vehicles attached to a unit.

Replacement Depot (later called Reinforcement Depot) – transit camp for personnel awaiting assignment.

Repple Depple – slang for Replacement Depot.

Special Service – Education and Entertainment section responsible for the morale of troops on a base.

War Bonds – debt securities issued by a government to finance military operations and other expenditure in times of war.

Appendix 1

US Units Stationed in Stone

2nd WAC Separate Battalion (September 1943)
6th Convalescent Hospital (March 1944)
7th Medical Lab
8th Air Force Replacement Depot (March-August 1944)
14th Replacement Control Depot (September 1943-August 1944)
16th Replacement Control Depot (September 1943-August 1944)
18th Replacement Control Depot (March 1944-August 1944)
19th Replacement Control Depot (March 1944-August 1944)
29th Postal Regulating Section (August 1944-May 1945)
34th Medical Battalion (April 1944-August 1944)
35th Evacuation Hospital (March 1944)
37th Medical Battalion
64th Medical Group (March 1944)
65th US Army Band (April 1944)
66th Medical Group (March 1944)
67th Medical Group (March 1944)
70th Replacement/Reinforcement Depot (December 1944-1945)
93rd Station Complement Squadron (April 1944-May 1945)
129th Replacement Battalion (December 1944-May 1945)
130th Replacement Battalion (December 1944-May 1945)
130th General Hospital (August 1944-September 1944)
131st Army Postal Unit (August 1944-staging)
132nd Replacement Battalion (December 1944-May 1945)
133rd Replacement Battalion (December 1944-May 1945)
145th Army Postal Unit (April 1944)
153rd Replacement Battalion (December 1944-May 1945)
154th Replacement Battalion (December 1944-May 1945)

155th Replacement Battalion (December 1944-May 1945)
156th Replacement Battalion (December 1944-May 1945)
157th Replacement Battalion (December 1944-May 1945)
158th Replacement Battalion (December 1944-May 1945)
162nd Replacement Battalion (December 1944-May 1945)
163rd Replacement Battalion (December 1944-May 1945)
164th Replacement Battalion (December 1944-May 1945)
165th Replacement Battalion (December 1944-May 1945)
166th Replacement Battalion (December 1944-May 1945)
167th Replacement Battalion (December 1944-May 1945)
169th Medical Battalion (April 1944-May 1944)
171st Medical Battalion
173rd Medical Battalion (April 1944)
174th Medical Battalion (February 1944-July 1944)
182nd Medical Battalion (August 1944)
205th Medical Dispensary, Aviation (December 1944)
405th Quartermaster Air Depot Platoon (September 1943)
429th Collection Company (April 1944)
437th Collection Co. (March 1944)
438th Collection Co. (April 1944-August 1944)
510th Clearing Company (April 1944)
513th Clearing Company (April 1944)
535th Clearing Company (April 1944)
559th Clearing Company (April 1944)
561st Army Postal Unit (September 1943-November 1944)
581st Army Postal Unit (April 1944)
610th Clearing Company
666th Clearing Company
695th Army Air Force Band (May 1945)
831st Quartermaster G.S. Company (December 1944)
832nd Quartermaster G.S. Company (December 1944)
890th Army Postal Unit (May 1945)
891st Army Postal Unit (May 1945)
921st Ordnance Heavy Auto Maintenance Company (December 1944)

1257th MP Company, Aviation (August 1943-1945)
1727th Ordnance Medium Maintenance Company (February 1944-April 1944)
2069th Quartermaster Truck Company, Aviation (April 1944-May 1944)
3445th Ordnance Medium Battalion (April 1944-July 1944)

- Units are in numerical order, rather than date order.
- Dates show when units are known to have been there. They could have been there for longer periods.
- Possibly some units only had some detachments at Stone – rather than the entire outfit.
- Some units changed their designation to a different unit – where this is known it is noted.
- Some units were based at a number of camps around Stone.

Appendix 2

US Units Stationed in Chorley

12th Replacement Control Depot (September 1943-March 1944)
94th Station Complement Squadron (March 1944-May 1945)
127th Replacement Battalion, AAF (May 1945)
150th Replacement Company (December 1944-May 1945)
151st Replacement Company (December 1944-May 1945)
152nd Replacement Company (December 1944-May 1945)
302nd Gas Defence Detachment (September 1943-March 1944)
405th Quartermaster Air Depot Platoon (September 1943)
580th Ambulance Company, Motorised (August 1944)

- Units are in numerical order, rather than date order.
- Dates show when units are known to have been there. They could have been there for longer periods.
- Possibly some units only had some detachments at Chorley – rather than the entire outfit.
- Some units changed their designation to a different unit – where this is known it is noted.
- Some units were based at a number of camps around Chorley.

Appendix 3

US Units Stationed in Bamber Bridge

159th Replacement Company, Air Force (May 1945)
160th Replacement Company, Air Force (May 1945)
205th Medical Dispensary, Aviation (May 1945)
1511th Quartermaster Truck Battalion (June 1943-September 1943)
1513th Quartermaster Truck Battalion (September 1943)
1514th Quartermaster Truck Battalion (September 1943)
2054th Quartermaster Truck Company, Aviation (September 1943)
2055th Quartermaster Truck Company, Aviation (September 1943)
2057th Quartermaster Truck Company, Aviation (September 1943)

- Units are in numerical order, rather than date order.
- Dates show when units are known to have been there. They could have been there for longer periods.
- Possibly some units only had some detachments at Bamber Bridge – rather than the entire outfit.
- Some units changed their designation to a different unit – where this is known it is noted.
- Some units were based at a number of camps around Bamber Bridge.

Appendix 4

US Units Stationed in Keele

18th Replacement Control Depot
31st Anti-Aircraft Artillery Group (August 1944)
45th Anti-Aircraft Artillery Group (August 1944)
56th Anti-Aircraft Artillery Brigade (August 1944)
74th Anti-Aircraft Artillery Brigade (August 1944)
83rd Infantry Division (April-June 1944)
559th Anti-Aircraft Artillery A.W. Battalion, mobile (August 1944)
787th Anti-Aircraft Artillery A.W. Battalion, semi-mobile (August 1944)
788th Anti-Aircraft Artillery A.W. Battalion, semi-mobile (August 1944)
791st Anti-Aircraft Artillery A.W. Battalion, semi-mobile (August 1944)
2096 Quartermaster Truck Company, Avn
3804 Quartermaster Truck Company (March 1944)

- Units are in numerical order, rather than date order.
- Dates show when units are known to have been there. They could have been there for longer periods.
- Possibly some units only had some detachments at Keele – rather than the entire outfit.
- Some units changed their designation to a different unit – where this is known it is noted.
- Some units may have been based at a number of camps around Keele.

Appendix 5

USSTAF Map

Map showing USSTAF in the UK June 1944. (Army Air Forces in WW2 – Craven and Cate)

Appendix 6

Red Cross Clubs Map

Map showing American Red Cross Clubs in the UK September 1943. (Fold 3)

Appendix 7

Jefferson Hall Sites Map

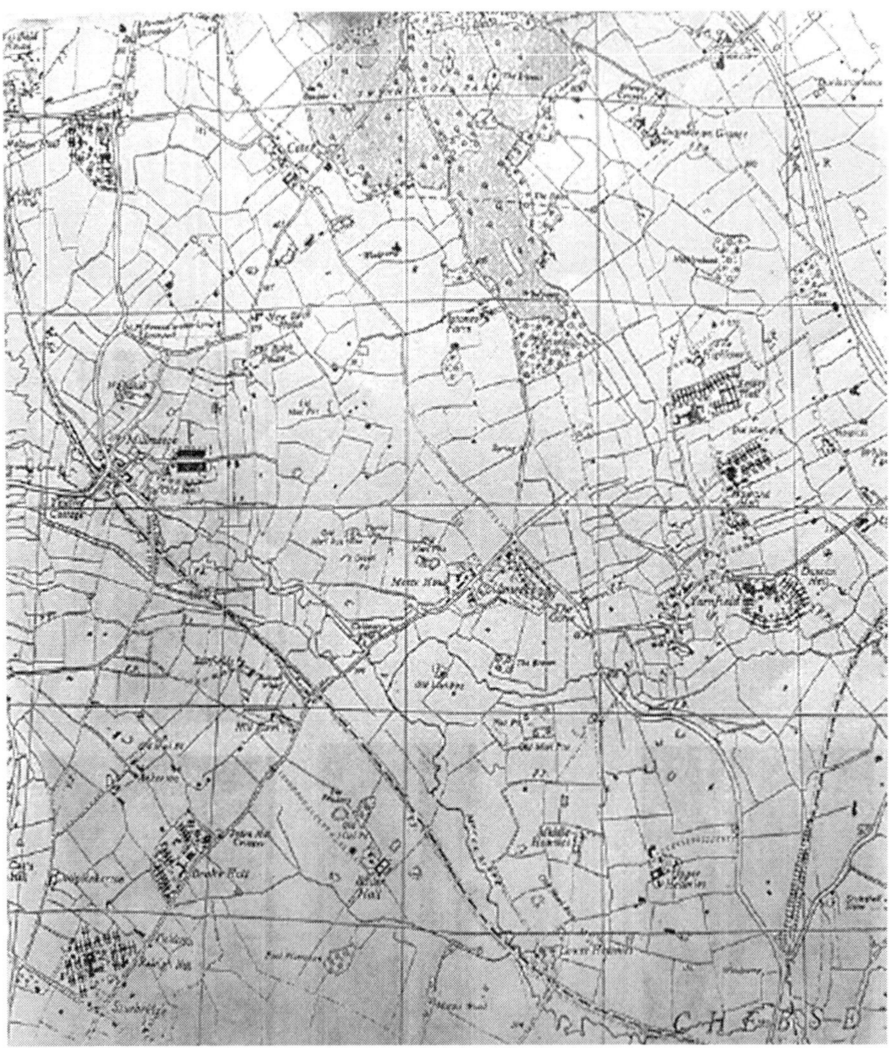

Map showing all four sites of Jefferson Hall: Beatty, Howard, Duncan and Nelson.

Appendix 8

Duncan Hall Map

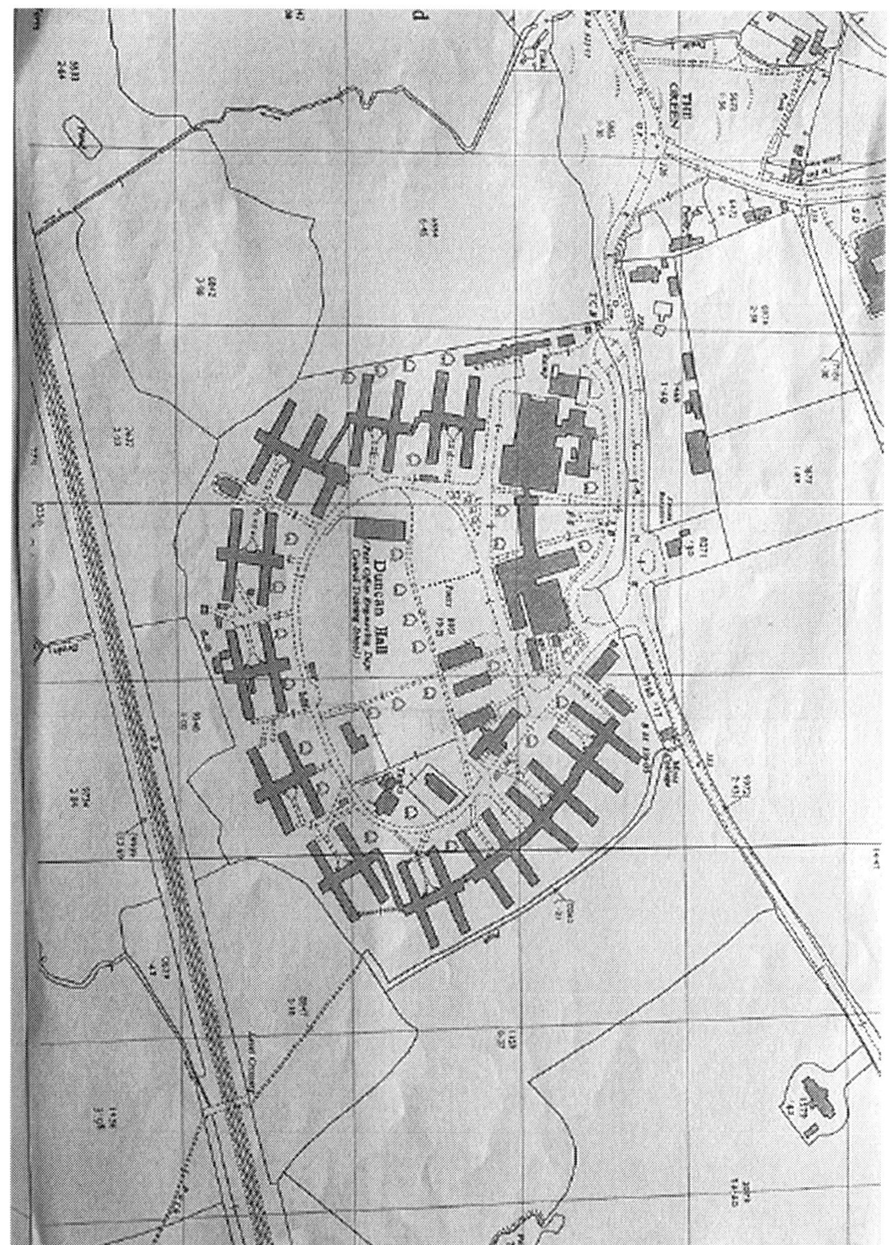

Aerial map of Duncan Hall. (Staffordshire Record Office, 1964)

Appendix 9

Beatty and Howard Hall Map

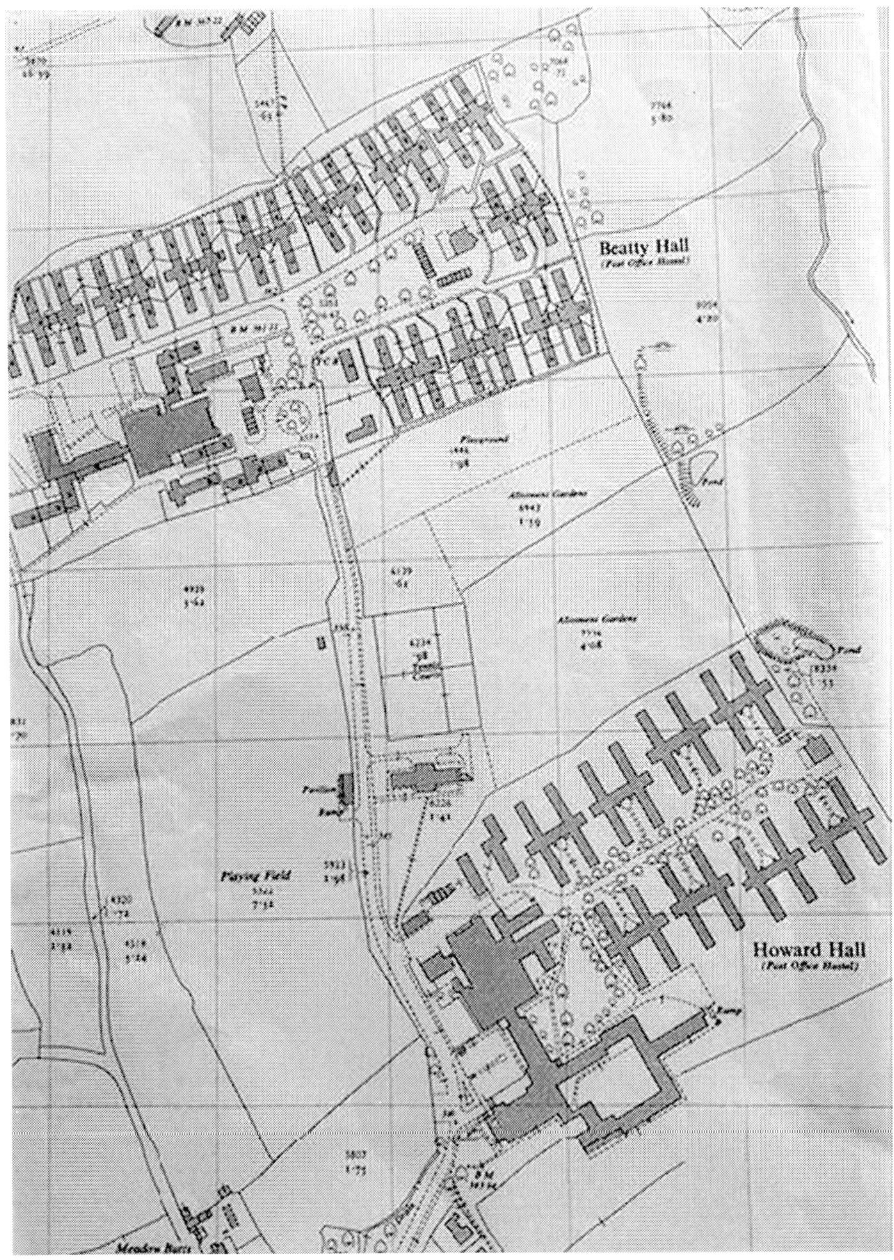

Aerial map of Beatty and Howard Hall. (Staffordshire Record Office, 1964)

Appendix 10

AAF Reinforcement Command

Organizations Assigned to AAF Reinforcement Command

	Officers & WO	Enlisted Men	Total
Headquarters, 70th Reinforcement Depot (AAF)	30	164	194
127th Reinforcement Bn (AAF)	21	116	137
128th Reinforcement Bn (AAF)	21	116	137
129th Reinforcement Bn (AAF)	21	116	137
130th Reinforcement Bn (AAF)	21	116	137
131st Reinforcement Bn (AAF)	21	116	137
132nd Reinforcement Bn (AAF)	21	116	137
133rd Reinforcement Bn (AAF)	21	116	137
134th Reinforcement Bn (AAF)	21	116	137
2069th QM Truck Co	3	99	102
208th Medical Dispensary	3	13	16
695th AAF Band	1	28	29
Bulk Allotment:			
93rd Station Complement Squadron Reinforcement Depot (Sp)	16	345	361
94th Station Complement Squadron Reinforcement Depot (Sp)	25	142	167
381st Station Complement Squadron Reinforcement Depot (Sp)	20	128	148
Totals	266	1847	2113

Encl #A

SECRET

Organisations assigned to AAF Reinforcement Command. (Fold 3)

Appendix 11

US Rest Homes

ACTIVATION OF REST HOMES

STATION

AAF 523 — Coombe House - Placed under the command jurisdiction of CO, 12th Replacement Control Depot, Per: par 1, GO 15, VIII AFSC (Secret) dtd 13 Sept 1943.

AAF 511 — Moulsford Manor - Placed under the command jurisdiction of CO, 12th Replacement Control Depot, Per: par 1, GO 24, VIII AFSC (Secret) dtd 17 August 1943.

AAF 593 — Stanbridge Earls - Placed under the command jurisdiction of CO, 12th Replacement Control Depot, Per: par 1, GO 24, VIII AFSC (Secret) dtd 17 August 1943.

AAF 503A — Roke Manor - Activated with Detachment A, 133rd Replacement Bn AAF, Per par 17, SO 19, Hq 8th AFSC dtd 19 January 1944.

AAF 511A — Bucklands - Activated with Detachment B, 133rd Replacement Bn AAF, Per: par 17, SO 19, Hq 8th AFSC dtd 19 January 1944.

AAF 558 — Walhampton House - Activated with Detachment D, 133rd Replacement Bn AAF Per par 17, SO 19, Hq 8th AFSC dtd 19 January 1944.

AAF 556 — Aylesfield House - Activated with Detachment E, 133rd Replacement Bn AAF, Per par 25, SO 52, Hq 8th AFSC dtd 22 February 1944.

AAF 557 — Pangbourne House - Activated with Detachment F, 133rd Replacement Bn AAF Per par 22, SO 98, Hq 8th AFSC dtd 7 April 1944.

AAF 562 — Spetchley Park - Activated with Detachment G, 133rd Replacement Bn AAF Per: par 23, SO 128, Hq 8th AFSC dtd 8 May 1944.

AAF 563 — Furze Down House - Activated with Detachment H, 133rd Replacement Bn AAF Per: par 34, SO 159, Hq 8th AFSC dtd 7 June 1944.

AAF 498 — Ebrington Manor - Activated with Detachment I, 133rd Replacement Bn per: par 43, SO 161, Hq 8th AFSC dtd 10 June 1944.

AAF 566 — Keythorp Hall - Activated with Detachment K, 133rd Replacement Bn AAF Per: par 28, SO 166, Hq 8th AFSC dtd 15 June 1944.

AAF 567 — Eynsham Hall - Activated with Detachment L, 133rd Replacement Bn AAF Per: par 16, SO 176, Hq 8th AFSC dtd 25 June 1944.

AAF 524 — Birkdale Palace Hotel - Activated with Detachment M, 133rd Replacement Bn Per: par 25, SO 243, Hq 8th AFSC dtd 1 Sept 1944.

AAF 474 — Phyllis Courts - Activated with Detachment O, 133rd Replacement Bn Per: par 11, SO 244, Hq 8th AFSC dtd 23 Sept 1944.

AAF 495 — Knight Shayes - Activated with Detachment N, 133rd Replacement Bn Per: par 20, SO 257, 8th AFSC dtd 14 Sept 1944.

Incl #10 ~~SECRET~~

Activation of US Rest Homes. (Fold 3)

By the Same Authors

Letters for Victory,
ISBN 978-1-85858-016-6, £10.95

Somewhere in the Midlands,
ISBN 978-1-85858-119-4, £6.95

They Also Serve Who Stand And Wait,
ISBN 978-1-85858-204-7, £9.95

Camp Foxley,
ISBN 978-1-85858-285-6, £10.95

Blackmore Park in World War Two,
ISBN 978-1-85858-428-7, £10.95

Return to Duty,
ISBN 978-1-85858-454-6, £10.95

The Friendly Invasion of Leominster,
ISBN 978-1-85858-493-5, £12.95

Bridging The Gap,
ISBN 978-1-85858-525-3, £10.95

U.S. Army Hospital Center 804,
ISBN 978-1-85858-565-9, £12.95

Keep 'em Rollin', Keep 'em Shootin', Keep 'em Supplied,
ISBN 978-1-85858-712-7, £12.95